Business Promotion Techniques

A Marketer's Guide to Improving Your Business Visibility and Increasing Customer Engagement

Ralf Percy

Table of Contents

Book Description

A Marketer's Guide to Improving Your Business Visibility and Increasing Customer Engagement

Promoting your business requires a fine balance between your business goals and the resources available at your disposal. Many times, we deny our businesses and the opportunity to thrive because we fear the unknown. Nothing should hold you back. Marketing today has evolved so much such that even with limited resources, you can still work wonders for your business.

In this book, we take an in-depth look at some of the significant promotional strategies you can use today to boost your profile, improve your business visibility, and increase engagement with your customers.

The techniques discussed in this book demystify the financial constraint myth that hinders many businesses from reaching their potential. A lot of the methods discussed can be leveraged online especially through social networking. We have examined in-depth multiple procedures, risks, benefits, and where applicable, useful tips to help you start from scratch and grow your business.

As you work toward promoting your business, remember that there exists a fine line between your business and your customers. Build your strategies with your customers in mind. After all, it is their approval you seek to grow sales and make your business a household name.

Introduction

Getting the right promotional mix is one of the many challenges that businesses struggle with. Most times, promotional and marketing strategies go hand in hand. Business promotion is all about information sharing. You need to ensure your customers are aware of your products, the price, or any other unique offering that you have.

While it is common knowledge that for any business to thrive, you must promote it adequately. Every business owner has specific reasons why they expand their business at a given point in time; however, these reasons go beyond simply monetary gains. One of the most important things you should get from promoting your business is healthy customer engagement as building and maintaining healthy relationships with your customers is what will ensure that business grows in leaps and bounds over the years.

Customer loyalty doesn't come easy. It is a value proposition where you offer the customer a guaranteed value, and in return, they stay loyal to your brand. In a market where customer tastes and preferences are so dynamic, you always need to be at the top of your game, knowing everything about ongoing market trends, anticipating any future customer needs, and more in order to survive and thrive.

Promotional and marketing strategies often tend to coincide, to the point where some people struggle to tell the difference between the two. Marketing generally focuses on the development and proliferation of your business to customers. On the other hand, promotion is all about communication. Once the products are in the market, it is wise to communicate the specificity of your products to your target audience.

Customers might be aware of your products already, but they are also aware of other brands/businesses whose products or services meet their needs in a similar manner. So, *what* is it about your business that captivates them, holds their attention, and continues to make them ignore others? This is where promotional communication comes in. Promotion is about research and development. It should be a long-term plan that allows room for revision to meet your current needs.

Think of promotional strategies like the notification messages on your phone. You have a lot of apps installed, and several accounts that are linked to them. You might not have the time to access all the apps, so instead, you receive notifications whenever something new or important happens. These are reminders that you need to check the app or respond in some way. Promotional strategies do the same thing. They remind customers of your existence. More importantly, they ensure your customers the value they get from your business.

A world of business without promotion is unimaginable. You would simply have some amazing products or services that no one knows about. This beats the purpose of running a business in the first place. For most companies, the initial promotion strategies are built around personal selling, communicating or increasing sales. However, the longer you stay in the business, the more you need to refine your promotional approach to ensure your business strategy evolves with customer tastes and preferences. As the business grows, you start remodeling your promotional strategies around things like venturing into new territories, increasing your market share or diversification. The underlying factor behind these strategies is effective communication.

Promotion should be an essential part of your business. Take a moment and think about some of the brands we interact with today. Global brands like Coca-Cola have been around since you were young, yet they still keep spending billions on promotion. You see their ads everywhere, from billboards to social media ads. For a company as successful as they are, why is it that they keep advertising their product even though they are already ahead of the game? The lesson here is that you never stop promoting your business. It is an endless process.

The Coca-Cola ads that used to appeal to you as a child probably won't derive the same attention from you today, other than nostalgia. The same ads might not evoke any reaction from your kids. The company realizes the demographic dynamics in their target audience; that's why they keep reinventing ads every other time. They have unique ads around Christmas, Easter, and for every occasion day in the calendar year. Strategies like these are the reason why they are so popular. They might be selling sodas, but at the same time, you will not walk into a nightclub, for example, and ask for a Pepsi cocktail. This is how elaborate their reach is.

As long as you have a long-term perspective of your business, you must see business promotion as a life-long process. Product development, new research, and rejuvenating your promotional strategies will go a long way in helping you set your business on the road to success. The other lesson is that life goes on. Everything around us is in a state of motion. Your customers might be excited about a campaign you did a while back, but they are more concerned about what you are doing now, and your next move. Business does not reward complacency; you can never rest easy. You have to be active in promoting your business. You must think outside the box all the time.

What do you stand to gain from creating excitement about your brand? Think about promotion as a five-prong strategy as follows:

First, we have to develop brand awareness among the audience. Promoting your business will help you create and manage customer anticipation. There are several strategies that you can use to create conversations around your brand. As you do this, you must also think in terms of consistency. Build your brand naturally so that your customers can feel they are not being coerced into doing business with you.

Next, you have to think about attracting traffic to your business. Eventually, promotion is a game of numbers. You do expect to see an improvement in different kinds of traffic. From online conversations to purchases, if you run your promotion well, you should expect an uptake in interest. Don't take this for granted either. When you get attention from customers, appreciate them back by making them feel welcomed, special, and a part of your journey.

Third, your promotional input should help your customers toward effective decision-making. You need decisive and proactive customers who will respond to your promotional content in the desired manner. To support this cause, provide them with actionable information. Build a promotional strategy that provides them with valuable input which will help them realize your value proposition.

Fourth, your promotional strategy should encourage customers to purchase or make an offer. This means that you are looking toward boosting your profits from sales. So how do you go about it? What should you do to make the customers choose you over everyone else? The answer to these questions will depend on the nature of your business, but it is a statement(s) that should guide your promotional strategy. You might be looking at giveaways or discount offers, freemium membership services or any other incentive you have to entice the customers.

Finally, your promotional strategy should prop your marketing tactics. You should align these two areas so that you have a year-long calendar to guide your approach. Remember, success in one of them should boost success in the other because they go hand in hand. Obviously, your promotional strategy will influence your marketing schedule, so ensure your marketing team is well-informed about this, and more importantly, their role going forward.

There are different kinds of input that will guide your promotional strategy, depending on your market, industry or niche. However, one thing that you must heavily rely on is data. There is a lot of data around, especially if you have a website. Customers engage with you from time to time on your website and social media pages, during which they share useful data. Use this to help you map the way forward for your promotional strategies.

As you look into promoting your business, remember that there is no business too small or too large to benefit from the promotion. Strategies might be different in terms of scalability, scope, and budget, but you are essentially doing the same thing regardless of the size of your business. Understand your market, the competition, and the demographics of your target audience. Once you have these three elements in check, you can work on a promotional approach specially tailored to suit your needs.

"The greatest thing to be achieved in advertising, in my opinion, is believability, and nothing is more believable than the product itself."

– Leo Burnett

Chapter 1
How to Use Flyers and Posters to Promote Your Business

"You can't use up creativity. The more you use, the more you have."

– Maya Angelou

Promotion is one of the important things you think about concerning your business. Effective promotion strategies are at the center of your business. Whether yours is a small, medium-sized or large business, you must have a promotion strategy that aligns with your long-term growth strategy. Flyers and posters have been used by many companies over the years and prove to be effective promotional tools even today.

Flyers and posters are useful and practical options for your business because they are scalable. They are very easy to create. Even with the simplest posters, you must still be creative in your design. Why is it that these mundane tools are essential for promotional purposes?

For many years, flyers and posters have been used for business promotion because of their effectiveness in delivering the advertiser's information to customers. As much as people are heavily reliant on social media today, flyers and posters still retain their role in business promotion. They are the show stoppers and will always grab your attention.

Think about your recent encounter with flyers or posters, for example. You might not have intended to check them out, but when you came across them, you could not pass up the chance. The way they grab attention is one of the reasons why these age-old techniques are still in use today, and thriving.

Another reason why you should consider using posters and flyers is that you can design them to suit your budget. Startups with a limited budget can benefit from this technique in that you can create them without spending a lot. With basic graphic design skills, you can easily create some catchy flyers and distribute them to your audience wherever you feel suitable.

Importance of Posters and Flyers

Versatility is one of the benefits you get from using flyers and posters for your business. For the value of your money, it doesn't get any better than this. Listed below are some reasons why posters and flyers are still one of the best ideas you can consider for promoting your business today.

- Brand awareness

One of the first things many people do today whenever they need to find information about a product or service it to research online. This is a constant decision-making process. Many people cannot explain why they prefer checking for product or brand information online because they have gotten used to this trend; it is almost natural.

However, you can tap into this and create awareness for your brand. While people fancy online searches, a localized solution sounds even better. People appreciate your business better when you can provide immediate solutions and suggestions to their problems. Flyers are, therefore, a good way to build a name for your business in the community.

- Strategic marketing

Posters and flyers are a proper technique to target specific audience. Since they are easy to distribute, you can design them with a unique message along with some added incentive for the customer. When you think about the alternatives, such as the print media, which is very expensive, flyers and posters are more effective.

Say you are targeting a mature religious crowd, for example. You would distribute flyers and posters over the weekends around religious places. You will have a better chance of getting positive responses and feedback that way than using other means. For a local business, most of the people you target will be well-known to you, so convincing them would be a tad bit easier given the know-like-trust factor already in place.

- Affordability

There is always the argument in terms of cost-effectiveness, and in this regard, posters and flyers are a sure winner. You can design and print your own flyers and posters at home. Even if you hire an expert to do it for your business, it still would not cost you as much as you would spend on other promotional techniques.

- Simplicity

You can spend months working on some promotional strategies and tools. Flyers and posters, on the other hand, can be ready for distribution in a few hours from the moment you started printing them. Most people have them ready in a day or less, especially if the design is well-planned already.

Other than the ease of production, the simplicity in flyers and posters is another benefit your business will enjoy. You can choose to include as much or little information as you feel necessary in them. Therefore, you don't run the risk of confusing your audience or overwhelming them with information. A few catchy words in the right font and some good graphics, coupled with creative color selection will have your promotional content appealing to your audience.

- Introduce incentives

If you are thinking of incentivizing your business in some way, flyers and posters are an excellent way to go. People who have them will probably be talking about the 50% discount offer at your store. They are good for gaining interest and could work well to help you create awareness for your business.

- Palpability

One of the highlighted benefits of using flyers and posters is that they are palpable. Your audience can carry it with them wherever they go. This works well for you because your message can reach a lot more people than you had planned. If someone is traveling and they carry your posters with them, there's a good chance someone in their destination will get your message and think about it.

How many times have you received flyers at the mall, and ended up with them on your coffee table at home? A message that was dispatched through you ends up being received by everyone in your household, and all this is through one flyer.

While there are strong claims from individuals and businesses about the rise of promotional content on social media and its benefits, do not ignore what you can achieve with flyers and posters. They might seem outdated for the modern customer, but at times it is the old-fashioned techniques that still work best. Remember that you must be creative in your design to get the best results.

How to Design the Best Flyers and Posters

Flyers and posters are still winning, so many years after they were first used for promotional purposes. Even in the face of technology and social media where many traditional forms of marketing are struggling, flyers and posters are still leaving an impact. When you think of these tools, most people limit their ideas to the physical flyers and posters they come across in the neighborhood. This is a great idea. However, you can also create the same for online use, share them on social media, emails, or post them on your website. There are endless ways of using flyers and posters for promotional purposes, which makes them quite a spectacle in marketing and advertising today.

These tools have remained iconic in promotion over the years because of their dynamic graphic approach. For decades, companies have used flyers and posters to promote events, sales, or even invite people to a cause. In a world where your chances of coming across brochures and other means of advertisements are as high as meeting a stranger, it is not easy to come up with designs that will attract your audience and keep them hooked. Bearing that in mind, let's look at some useful tips to help you design some fantastic promotional content for your business.

- Be the audience

The first mistake that many people make when designing posters and flyers is to think about their own perspective. You have to change your vantage point. Put yourself in the audience. Assume you are the customer – what would you want to see? What message would attract you to the business? If you are unable to do this, it might help to think about one of your favorite businesses, for example. What is it that draws you to them? How do you find their posters?

If you can, brainstorm with someone and share your ideas with them. This is a good idea because you will learn so much from them. The design is not for you; it is for your customers. You have to be very careful when considering the kind of information you put in the flyers and the mode of communication. Cartoon action figure designs are a good way to attract children, which means their parents will have no other option but to bring them to your store.

- Call to action

Designs without a call to action are useless. A call to action is that one thing you want the customer to do once they see your poster or flyer. Do you need them to sign up, make a purchase or contact you? This is something so essential yet you will come across many leaflets and posters that don't have it. A call to action gives your design a purpose.

Assume you have been in the business for years, and you need to know more about your audience's views about your business; you would need honest reviews. Your flyers and posters should incorporate this message. Do not scream it out, however. Be subtle about it, but make it prominent.

While at it, be careful not to confuse your audience. We have seen many brochures that contain more than one call to action. There's a common unwritten rule in web design that your website must load in less than three seconds. If someone has to wait longer than three seconds to load, they will probably move on to something else. The same applies to your flyer design. People should get the point in a few seconds, or they will be lost and miss the point altogether.

- Colors, themes, and fonts

Creativity in design will go a long way in helping you achieve your promotional objectives for your promotional plans. You have thousands of color schemes, themes and font styles that you can use for your design. The problem here is that this variety can leave you spoilt for choice. This is the kind of nightmare that many designers have to deal with.

Given all the choices available, at times, it is wise to go simple. If you are undecided, start with the basic options. Basic primary colors are an excellent place to begin. Once you have the work in process, you can tinker around with different hues, layouts, and design elements.

You can also use your business brand as a guiding principle to determine what the best color choice is for your flyers. Focus on the content flow. Using more than two fonts in your design will probably create chaos in your production. If your design is targeting kids, primary colors are always a good option. If you are targeting a professional audience, you have to be bold in your design. Using white and black shades is always a good way to deliver that classy professional touch.

- Message clarity

Get to the point. Just like a call to action, your message should be clear to the audience in a few seconds. To make this easier, use some visual cues to help the audience. Choose the right graphics, place the intended message in the correct position. You want the message to be clear and unmissable. If you want the customer to contact you, they don't have to keep looking for your contact information. Put it in a section where they can see it.

While you work on this, remember value addition is important too. Indeed, you need the customer to get in touch. The question you should answer is why? Why should they contact you? Just dropping your contact information is not good enough. Show them what they benefit from contacting you and your inbox and phones will be blowing up.

- Maintain professionalism

Professionalism is not a preserve for big businesses. As long as you are asking people to invest their time and resources in your business, they expect you to be professional about it too. Professionalism in flyer and poster design involves a lot of things. Start with the photos you choose, for example. Use high-quality photos. Invest in a good camera, or hire an expert to handle production for you.

Today you can go online and use high-quality stock photos to enhance your design. At the same time, remember that stock photos might not always be a good idea because some people feel they lack the personal touch or fall short in originality. Whichever option you choose, always remember that a professional design is a great way to enhance your business profile.

- Creative distribution

It is pointless to design amazing promotional content when you cannot distribute them effectively. The design process doesn't end when you print your content; you must be creative in distribution too. There are lots of avenues you can use for this. Think about the audience because it will affect your budget too. If you have a large audience, your costs will be higher if you choose mail distribution. Instead, online distribution will cut costs, and even help you reach a wider audience.

If you choose to send the flyers through email, don't just upload the flyer and send. Reconsider the design. Test it on a temporary email to see how it displays on different browsers. Try it on your phone and tablet too. Whatever you do, make sure the final copy you send to your customers is perfect.

Tips for Effective Distribution

Your design is perfect, your message is clear and everything about your pamphlets meets your promotional objectives. You have them printed and ready for distribution. This is the last step in bringing your customers closer to the business. Don't give up now; you're almost there. For all the input you have put into this project, it would be sad to fail at the last step.

Distribution is just as important as the design process. You have the message ready; now you just need to get it to the right people. You have to be creative in the distribution process to ensure your flyers get to the right people. We have seen several cases where flyers are strewn all over the streets, but no one pays attention to them. This is no more than littering and is an environmental nuisance. You might as well find yourself in a fit with the law. Just as creative and precise as you have been during the design process, you must follow the same procedure in distribution.

The following are some useful distribution tips that will help you get your flyers to the right people:

● Send to mailboxes

You can personally send the flyers to customer mailboxes. This is good if you have a niche market and you know who your target audience is. If this is not the case, you could end up with a tedious delivery process, sending brochures to every mailbox in your neighborhood.

Instead of going through all that trouble, why don't you email them instead? Find their email addresses and reach millions of inboxes in seconds by sending just one email. Better yet, share it on your social media platform and you will reach just as many people in a short time.

● Package inserts

Package inserts are another option to send flyers. In many cases, you can do it blindly and hope to get some responses. Many times, you purchase your daily newspaper and find pamphlets inside. These have nothing to do with the newspaper, but they will still get your attention. Perhaps there's a new store that opened up in your neighborhood that is giving away insane discounts. You will probably check it out when you are running some errands, as will many other people. The flyers could also remind you of a purchase you have been putting off for a while, whereby you now end up completing your purchase as a result.

- Business partners

You don't have to go it all alone. You can consult other business partners around and ask them to display your flyers in their premises. This is a good idea if you have a good relationship with them already. They can display your leaflets on their counters, and in return, you do the same for them when their time comes.

Talk to the management of the local hospitals, hotels, restaurants and any other public place where you are bound to get lots of human traffic. This kind of partnership is good and will go a long way in strengthening your ties with other local businesses, thereby expanding your network.

- Event distribution

Another good place for you to distribute flyers is at events. Luckily, there's a lot happening all the time in most towns. As you look for events where you can distribute flyers, think about the audience too. Having flyers in the wrong place can lead to ridicule and make you the laughing stock. It's like going to an atheist event to distribute flyers for a Christian fellowship program.

Some event managers can allow you to have a stand at their reception for your business. Here you can do more than just share your flyers; you can briefly discuss your business with the audience. Answer some questions, ask some of your own. The engagement will prop your promotional strategy. If you have some goodies to distribute, have them prepared and packed in neat presentable goodie bags alongside the flyers.

- Timely distribution

Timing is another important factor you must consider. Look at it this way; flyers are paper prints, other than those you distribute online. Paper prints generally do not have a long shelf life. If you are distributing them outdoors, their lifespan is considerably shorter thanks to the weather. In light of this, consider the weather before you start pinning them all over town. It would be unfortunate for you to pin all your flyers only for the rain to undo your work minutes after you are done.

Apart from the weather, think about the seasons too. If you are preparing flyers around Easter or Halloween, rest assured you are fighting for space with a lot of businesses. Your flyers might end up in a very crowded place they become insignificant and irrelevant. So, what should you do, give up? No. The holidays are a good time to send flyers out. You just need to change the tact. Since most stores are busy, this would be a good time to talk to other store owners about displaying your flyers on their counters.

● The delivery method

Your preferred mode of delivery will also affect results. Are you handing out flyers directly to customers, delivering them door-to-door or putting them up in high traffic areas? Whichever method you prefer, it will affect your distribution plan in some way.

How many flyers do you have? How long do you plan to distribute them? Do you have permission to distribute flyers randomly? You have to consider the policies governing flyer distribution practices in your neighborhood before you begin.

● Build a reliable distribution team

Distributing flyers can be a gruesome affair, especially if you are doing it on your own. Consider asking for help. You can reach out to family and friends, and depending on the size of your business, you might even have to hire a team of experts to assist. Whichever case, make sure your distribution team is highly motivated and well-compensated for doing the job. You need a team that is as enthusiastic about distributing the flyers as you are about your business. It would help to make sure they know more about your business too, so they can answer some questions if someone needs clarity.

Chapter 2
Building Successful and Engaging Contests for Your Business

"It was the secret to winning any contest, he said, in life or in the boxing ring — you just had to get up more than you fell down."

— *Kameron Hurley*

Contests are increasingly popular today. You will come across lots of contests on different social media platforms. While several people enter and engage in these contests, many don't realize it is more than the company engaging their customers and rewarding them, but a promotional strategy. Come to think about it, each time you participate in the contest, most of your conversations online and offline will be about the company and that contest. You might even encourage someone else to participate in the contest, hoping that they can win something.

Understanding Promotional Contests

Contest marketing is a technique that has worked for businesses for years. You have seen sweepstakes where people win brand-new vehicles, contracts, endorsements, vacations or even a new home. Contests are a psychological construct. That is why they are so effective.

The idea of winning something free at the end of the contest excites you, triggering your brain to produce oxytocin, the hormone that makes you feel happy. Your excitement increases the longer you participate in the competitions, and you might even go out of your way to purchase something to keep you in the running. After the contest is over, you may still end up discussing the company and the contest, or even look forward to more in the future.

Contests, therefore, are the kind of promotional strategy that will always guarantee more people engaging with your brand. Don't just think about contests as a strategy that top companies use; even small businesses can use it effectively. As a psychological construct, most competitions try to persuade customers to do something urgently. Since the customers are looking forward to gratification or some incentives that have been promised to them, they comply.

What do you gain from the contest? Well, depending on the information you request from the participants, you will have a lot of data that you can use for marketing purposes in the future. If the participants use their emails, you can add them to your mailing list and keep in touch whenever you have a new product coming up.

Many businesses struggle to get leads. There is no better way to get them than through contests. Not only do you receive useful data, you also have an audience that is eager for the next contest in case they don't win the current one. This level of anticipation is great for promoting your business.

When you plan a contest, do not limit your ideas to the contest. Incorporate other aspects of your business in the contest, especially your marketing needs. We have seen contests in the past where participants are asked questions about the company, the products or services and other detailed information. To answer accurately, they would have to learn more about the company. This way, you end up with a participant network that is well-informed about the business. Even if they didn't know more about your business, they will go out of their way to ensure they learn. In the process, they might also encourage others to learn, hoping to win.

Creating and Managing the Contest

Now that you know how contests work, let's discuss how to create one. Remember that the guiding principle behind your competition should be engagement. You don't just need participants, you need engaging participants.

● Identify the target audience

As you plan for the contest, make sure you have the right audience in mind. Don't just attract participants, go after your customers. These are the people who matter most to your business. Random participants might keep the contest lively, but they will not help your cause in the long run.

Research to know who your customers are, because this contest is for them. A general target audience will only keep the contest running, but will never translate into sales after the contest is over. Most of the participants might even block your contact details once they are done.

As you study and understand the audience, you must also realize that this contest should be about meeting their needs, interests, or solving some of their problems. If you can do this, you are one step closer to running a successful contest already.

● Set a budget

How much are you willing to invest in the contest? Yes, it is an investment. Think of the contest as a project you are investing in and focus on the end result. What do you intend to get out of the contest? From there, ask yourself how much you can comfortably set aside for the project. You are looking at a risk and return situation.

How do you tell whether the contest was a success? You have to define the goals and objectives of your contest from the beginning, and use this as a guideline for everything else that will follow. Are you looking for more followers? If so, how many followers?

Do you want to generate more traffic to your website? How much percentage increase are you targeting? What lessons will you draw from this? You can probably analyze the participation data to know the peak hours when your audience is active online. This will help in marketing your products or services in the future.

● Prior planning

Having defined the foundation and structure of your contest, you move on to strategizing. A contest must also be marketed. To gain sufficient traction, ensure people are aware of the contest.

If you plan on building the contest around a specific event or holiday like Christmas, make sure you market the content ahead of time. Work on the contest goals and map a plan of action.

In terms of planning, how frequently do you wish to run a contest? This will also depend on your budget. Most businesses do this at least four times a year. Quarterly contests allow you enough time to study the engagement data and have a working theory about your customers that you can use throughout the year. If your business is big enough, you can build on to have a contest every month. A monthly contest will definitely increase your engagement levels, and you could even identify your most loyal customers in the process.

- Choose the prize

About the prize, consider the one thing that will keep your participants excited. Of course, you cannot keep giving away all-expenses-paid holidays every month. However, if you are in the hotel industry, you could gift a lucky customer a free weekend each month of the year.

This point takes us back to our earlier assertion that contests are a psychological construct. The prize has to be something valuable and worth their participation, or your audience might soon get bored. Your competitors could also upstage you. You can also change things about in terms of the ultimate prize to keep things exciting.

- Type of contest

There are different types of competitions you can work with. For the best results, research well and settle on the best contest that would suit your audience, and meet your promotional needs at the same time. This decision will depend on what your audience appreciates. Think in terms of the kind of content that interests them, the holidays they look forward to, or the keywords that attract them. It is about managing their curiosity and using it to your advantage.

Consider a photo contest, where customers take photos with an item from your product line plus a catchy phrase and share it on your social media account. The most liked photo wins a prize. You can do the same with short videos. Another option is to use polls and surveys and have the participants voting to get one of them the ultimate prize. You could also simply ask questions and reward the first 10 people who get the answer right, or every 7th person to commemorate your 7th year in business.

- Rules and regulations

When managing a contest, you can rest assured that a lot of people will try to cheat. While you want to reward your loyal customers, you must consider one who truly deserves it. You will probably run your contest on a social media platform. To set you on the right path, make sure you read and understand each platform's guidelines for contest promotion. Without this, you could easily have the contest terminated or face a legal suit for breach of some guidelines. One of your participants might also sue if they realize they lost unfairly. This is not the kind of publicity you need.

Beyond the platform rules and regulations, you must also have some terms and conditions applicable to the contest. Highlight them and ensure they are easy to understand. Many people ignore terms and conditions because they barely have time to read the fine print. Make things easier and have few but straightforward rules as possible. It is an engaging social media contest, not a thesis.

- Contest promotion

The contest will not promote itself. It might be engaging, promising to reward winners with some amazing prizes, but it will not sell itself. Take the contest as a business product and give it the perfect launch. Have people talking about it. Give them something to get excited about. You can promote the contest through influencers on social media, email marketing, paid ads and any other option available to you.

- Data analysis

Each time you have a contest running, you are interacting with lots of participant data. Data is invaluable in the business world today, more so in marketing. You need to have some metrics embedded in your contest to deliver useful information about the contest in terms of customer participation.

For example, you might be interested in knowing how the customers learned about your business. What percentage of the participants gave their phone numbers hoping for follow-ups?

There is so much data you can get from contests, which can be used to inform your business decisions in the near future. Depending on your contest design, this is a good way to contact your customers directly about your business and their experience.

The points outlined above will help you create an awesome contest, one that should meet your promotional needs. At the back of your mind, you must never forget the psychological element of contest, and how to tweak things to your advantage. At the same time, be careful not to manipulate your audience. Contests are essentially about persuasion. Appeal to your customers' needs, and offer them value in exchange for their attention.

Benefits of Contest Promotion

Spend a few hours on Instagram, Twitter or Facebook and you will come across a lot of contests. These networks are the best place to engage existing and potential customers, hence the proliferation of contest marketing. You probably have participated in some contests before. You may or may not have been lucky, but one thing that probably keeps you engaged in contests is because of your affiliation with one of your favorite brands.

Social media contests are great for your business, especially if you do it well and effectively. The engagement with your customers is priceless. The following are some of the reasons why you should think about it, especially if you are still mulling over a promotion strategy.

● Establish your brand

While building your contest, ensure you allow participants to share the contest. The nifty share button will be useful as it allows the participants to spread the word about the business and the contest. When they share the contest, they are generating hype around your business and getting more people interested.

Businesses usually start their social media pages with a few hundred followers in the first few days or weeks. Through contests, they increase engagement and have more people liking or following their social media accounts. A few years down the line, most of the active followers also become active customers, making their purchases from the business all the time. You might be starting out as a small and relatively unknown brand, but don't let up yet. There's more in store for you if you promote your business properly.

● Build a community of customers

Contests bring people together in ways you would never imagine. Many times customers come across other participants in the contest and they are more excited because someone else is as excited about the contest as they are. This is the perfect platform for further discussions about your product, service or business beyond the contest.

In terms of building your unique community, a lot of people know very little about some companies or products until they participate in a contest. From there, they become loyal customers. It takes some businesses years to create a community of customers when you can do this in a few weeks by running a successful contest on social media.

Instead of businesses working hard to build their networks, they rely on customers to do the work for them, by endorsing their brands to their loved ones. Since they have been part of your experience with a product, it doesn't take much to sway their opinion either.

● Sales motive

Why are you running the contest? You will get lots of information about your customers, increase your audience base and many other reasons. However, the ultimate goal is usually to increase sales. Business is about making a profit, and you can do this by increasing sales, without changing anything in your current pricing model.

Contests introduce you to reliable leads which you can convert into valuable information. Contest winners are some of your best brand ambassadors because they might already have tried and tested your product to participate. Given their current situation, they will definitely come back for future purchases hoping to keep winning.

● Increase subscriptions

Another reason why contests are popular is because you can use them to grow your subscriber network. Allow customers to subscribe to your channels to participate in the contest. You can also offer forms for them to fill, which will supplement your lead generation needs.

The risk of sharing contact and personal information online is too high today. This has prevented many people from sharing or being cautious about sharing their information online. As you ask for contact information, make sure you have measures in place to safeguard the security and integrity of the customer's information.

Contests must be relevant to the customer, or it would be no different from spamming their emails. Customers today are very keen on products, services and brands that are relevant to them, and will easily block your messages or create filters to delete your messages automatically if they feel your approach doesn't serve their needs.

- Free marketing by your customers

Word of mouth is one of the most reliable forms of marketing. The audience relies on feedback about your brand from someone they trust or hold in high regard. This is why contests are a good fit for your business. Your current customers believe in the product since they have used it for years. From their experience, they can advise someone else to try your products too. It gets even better when the person they are recommending is using a different product but their experience is terrible.

- Incentivized approach to increase your followers

There are many ways of getting people to follow your social media accounts on different platforms. If you just created a social media page on Facebook for example, you can use your Twitter audience to grow the Facebook page.

A simple contest would involve the participants following a link on Twitter that redirects them to your Facebook page. They like the page and participate in the contest. This is a good way to grow your audience. Most of your followers on Twitter would probably follow on Facebook so they never miss out on any content you share. After all, they already love your brand.

● Create conversations about your products

One of the best ways to promote your business is to get people talking about it. The more people are talking about your business, the better for your brand. Contests are a good way to create such conversations. Online conversations are ideal because they generate quality organic traffic for your brand. From these conversations your brand can benefit from increased likes, retweets, followers and shares. These metrics will be useful for your marketing strategy in the future. Most of the people you engage in such discussions will stay around with you for a very long time, in the hope that they can learn more, and probably participate in future contests successfully.

● Cost effective marketing strategy

Compared to most of the other strategies you can use for marketing your business, contests are affordable. Even if you are operating on a limited budget, you can still promote your business. Other than that, contests create engagements around your brand that are worth the investment.

Sample Contest Ideas for Your Business

Contests on social media are a good way to encourage customers to engage with your brand. The conversations built around contests can push the limits of your business to unimaginable heights. There are different types of contests that you can use to further your promotional strategies. Let's discuss some of them below:

● Random surprise prizes

Many companies have used this strategy in the past, where they gift random customers from time to time. This usually happens in commemoration of some milestone that is dear to the company, like reaching 100,000 followers, a million subscribers or anything else that matters to the company. Since customers never expect these gifts or events, they will be happy to look forward to more in the future.

● Award creativity

Another strategy is to encourage customers to get creative with your brand and share their work. This can include photos or videos with your product either upon purchase or in use. You can have customers voting on the best submissions before you award the winners.

● Outlet check-ins

If you have multiple outlets, you can encourage your customers to share their check-in at different locations. After a specific duration, you will award one or a few of the lucky customers who participated.

● Rewarding feedback

Many people take feedback for granted. They assume that most companies never do anything about their feedback. To change their perception and encourage more engagement, reward some of your customers for their honest responses. You have to be careful with this one because some customers could easily try to exploit the system and share false responses.

● Trivia contests

Trivia contests are great in the sense that they encourage your customers to learn more about your brand. You can ask a series of questions that would need some research, then award some of the best responses.

● Best caption rewards

Upload a photo or video on social media and encourage your customers to get creative with their captions. You can choose the best captions and reward them or have the audience vote on the winning caption. The more engaging the process is, the better for you especially when the participants feel they are involved in choosing the ultimate winner.

The secret to running a successful contest on social media is to be transparent, honest and keep it as entertaining as possible. You need to dig into your creative juices to get this done.

Chapter 3
Using Samples and Giveaways to Drum Up Support for Your Business

"The excellence of a gift lies in its appropriateness, rather than in its value."

- *Charles Dudley Warner*

How many times have you gone shopping and ended up buying something other than the usual item you buy because the alternative had a gift attached to it? Many people do this. There are several reasons, but one of the common ones is the overall price. If you purchase item A and B separately, you spend $400. However, you can buy item A at $350 with item B bundled as a free gift. It makes sense that most people would take the cheaper offer.

Remember the excitement you had as a child when you found a surprise gift in your cereal box? That's the same excitement many people have when they receive free gifts with their purchases. In fact, many people end up changing their purchase preferences in anticipation of a free gift.

Gifts with purchases is a promotion strategy that has worked for years. For effectiveness, you must be particular about the gifts you offer customers. Some gifts are closely linked to the product or service on offer, while others are not. For example, a cigarette company could offer free ashtrays to their customers when they buy cigarettes from specific stores. This gift is directly linked to the purchase. An insurance company might offer free branded water bottles to customers who open accounts with them during a specific promotional window.

A gift with purchase is a common strategy that businesses use to gain a competitive advantage in the market. It is effective because other than enticing your current customers, you can also get other people to convert from their preferred brands and buy your products. One of the reasons why this method is preferred is because unlike other strategies, it adds value to the customer. The customer can spend less and still get the same value or higher.

People get excited about such promotional strategies because by design, they are often exclusive, and only run for a limited duration. Therefore, it introduces an element of urgency which will drive up sales. Many of the other promotional techniques cannot offer the same.

You might be looking at your gifts as a promotional strategy, but to the end user, it might mean so much more to them than you know. People appreciate products that cater to their needs intimately. This appreciative gesture might also endear the customer to your brand because they feel your business was there for them at their time of need.

Increasing Sales with Free Samples

It is not easy to find effective ways of attracting new customers. Every business owner strives to increase sales, especially when times are difficult. Given that there are so many strategies available already, how do you ensure free samples will help you increase sales and improve your business?

Before you begin, understand that this is another campaign. Like any other campaign, you must plan for it to the finest detail. You are looking for repeat sales, so you have to ensure your strategy meets the customer's needs. Here is a brief guideline to help you get it right:

- Successful launch

Think of the free gift strategy as launching a new product. What is your desired end result? Before dishing out gifts, make sure you have worked on your targets for the entire campaign. Other than issuing gifts, what else do you strive to achieve? By what percentage do you hope to increase sales? Perhaps you are offering gifts to clear dead stock or increase sales for a specific item in your store. How do you go about it?

In case your plan is to increase sales in general, a better idea would be to offer free gifts with any purchase in your store. This allows everyone to participate. By determining your ultimate goal, it is easier to estimate the effectiveness of the gift program throughout the duration of your campaign.

- Product appropriateness

It is okay to offer free gifts, but it is even better to offer gifts that are appropriate to the associated purchases, or the target audience. This calls for understanding your customers. Ideally, the gift should complement the product the customer is buying. If you sell cleaning products for utensils, scouring pads would make a good free gift because the customer will probably throw away their old scouring pads and use the new one.

● Terms and conditions

You must be clear about the terms associated with the free gifts. Customers need to know what they have to buy in order to enjoy the giveaway. Without this clarity, you might end up with disconcerted customers, and some might feel cheated. While at it, ensure they also know what they must do to enjoy the offer, what the offer is, how they will receive it, and more importantly, the duration of the offer.

● Perfect timing

An effective way of using the gift with purchase strategy is to plan it around a time when many people are shopping. Holidays are usually a good time for this. Other than timing the strategy, you might also have people buying things that they didn't really need, but since it is available for free, they buy them anyway. On timing, you must also ensure the product or service is appropriate with the specific duration you are offering the gifts.

● Brand your products

Since you stand to gain a lot of promotional mileage from this exercise, why not position your brand accordingly? This is a good time for you to remind the customers why your business is their best option in the market. Include your brand or your logo with the free gift. It might seem subtle, but the effect will linger in the minds of the customer for a very long time.

● Stock handling

Nothing spreads faster than bad news. People might be excited about the free samples on offer, but they will be twice as agitated when you run out of the free offers before they redeem their prizes, especially if they were within the limit of the promotional window. Check to ensure you have sufficient stock to cater to their needs. If you have to get daily deliveries from your supplier, make sure the supply schedule is appropriate so that you don't find yourself in a precarious situation with your customers.

● Determining success

How do you know if your strategy was a success or if it failed? You have to go back to the planning stage when launching your campaign. What were your goals? Have you achieved your targets? Do you need to extend the campaign or end it prematurely?

How to Use Free Samples Effectively

Free samples don't just help you clear stock, they also introduce reciprocity between your customers and your brand. It is human nature that whenever someone receives a gift, they almost feel obliged to do something in return. Buying from your store is an immediate form of reciprocity that you will definitely appreciate.

While free samples are a good way to promote your business, you must go about it with a plan. Without that, you might end up incurring losses and never getting any return on your investment. Let's discuss some brilliant ideas that will improve your chances of benefitting from the free samples below:

● Generating leads

Lead generation is one of a marketer's biggest concerns today. Free gifts can help you handle this effectively. You can request contact information from your customers in exchange for the free gifts. This way, you can follow up with the customers at a later data and have them commit to making immediate or future purchases.

- Product usability

The customer is always looking to maximize utility from their purchases. With this in mind, make sure you give them samples they can use everyday or frequently. This is a nifty trick that helps in brand positioning. You need them to engage with your product more often, which keeps it in their minds. The next time they go shopping, they could easily buy your products even without an offer.

- Target audience

Who is your intended recipient of the free samples? Think about it this way, it costs you a lot of money to avail the free gifts. Therefore, it would only make sense that you give them to people who find them useful, hence appreciate the gesture.

Giving gifts to the right people increases the chance that they will purchase from you, especially if your products served a key purpose in their lives. If you give gifts to anyone who comes into the store, you will be making a random investment and hoping that it pays off.

The best group to target should include your frequent customers and customers who have recently made purchases from your store. You could also offer gifts to potential customers, though you must carefully consider the demographics and ensure they meet your desired customer specifications.

- Value proposition

In as much as you are giving away free gifts, you must also ensure the gifts offer value to your customers. Value goes beyond the price of the item. Many people will look at gifts in terms of their monetary value, but those who seek deeper value in terms of utility will appreciate the product more.

● Surprise your customers

Imagine walking into your favorite store for a random everyday purchase and walking out with an amazing gift. Customers are often chuffed to bits by this. It is a strategy that can help you build or strengthen relationships with your customers. It gets even better of the surprise gift is something they need. For online stores, you probably have access to your customers' wishlists. Sending them something on their wishlist is a good way to have them loyal to your brand.

● Confidence boost

From time to time customers might have doubts about your products. This might be as a result of a negative or lots of negative reviews, or any other event that might have raised concerns about your brand. To counter this you can offer free products to help them overcome the negative perception.

It does not necessarily have to be a crisis situation that forces you into offering free gifts. You can also give away gifts when launching a new product so customers can try it and share their experience with you.

● Product positioning

Is there an event or seminar coming up that you are invited to? This is a good place to create a name for yourself. These events usually attract a lot of people, making them an ideal place to distribute free samples.

Depending on the nature of the event, you might also get the chance to converse with the recipients. Use this to answer some questions, ask them about their experience with the products they are currently using, what they feel could be improved in the product they are using, or in your products if they are already using them.

These events are generally crowded, so you need an offer that grabs everyone's attention. Position your product in a way that will have people talking about your brand at the event and beyond. Remember to socialize and leverage the event on social media too. The kind of conversations that come from this will be good for your brand.

Benefits of Using Free Samples

The idea of giving away free samples is something that many business owners dread. It is normal to be skeptical about getting returns from the gifts. The fact that you don't have a guaranteed return on investments further complicates the scenario. However, think about it — this is the same predicament that befalls marketers irrespective of the promotional technique they use. The idea, therefore, is to try and maximize on your promotional content so that you can get the best returns from your input.

Raising brand awareness is one of the ultimate goals of any promotional strategy. Free samples show customers that yours is a generous brand, and that you care for them. While you might look at it in terms of the money you invest in the gifts, you should also think about the benefits you stand to gain in the process.

When properly thought out, free gifts can help you improve your profile among your customers, and increase sales. Below are some reasons why you will benefit from free samples:

● Brand awareness

You have to think carefully about the products you are giving away for free. The reason for this is because people will talk about your products. Whether the conversations are positive or negative will depend on the product, and the way you present it to the customer. The fact is that those who receive the products will talk about them with their peers, friends and family members. The best way to stay ahead of the narrative is to perfect your product giveaway strategy.

● Customer reviews

While giving away free offers, reviews are probably the last thing on your mind, unless this was the intended purpose. When people receive a product for free, they are eager to use it and find out what makes it different from the others in the market, or anything that they are currently using.

Given the widespread use of marketing online, consider using a hashtag on the product label so that users can channel their reviews on the product through this. Reviews demand attention. Respond to as many of them as you can. This is a platform where you can engage customers and address their needs independently where possible.

Echo the positive customer feedback and endorsements by retweeting them if you use Twitter, and thank the customer. Follow up on the negative feedback too and address the customer's concerns. This will show customers that you care about their feedback.

● Brand stability

It would be absurd for a company that is struggling and on the verge of collapse to initiate a free gifts promotion strategy. Therefore, when you are giving away samples, people generally have the perception that you are a sound and financially stable company. Your generosity goes beyond the act of giving away free gifts. It is an assurance that your company will be there as a going concern for the foreseeable future. Yours is a brand that the customer can trust.

● Initiate current customers

If you have a product that is already in the market, you can entice your existing customers with a new line, or encourage them to spend more to enjoy additional benefits. They are already loyal to your brand, so it is easier to introduce them to a new product through giveaways. You can offer the free gifts with every purchase of their regular products, allowing them to enjoy what they normally use, and at the same time, sample your future products. The feedback from this will be useful not just for marketing purposes, but also for research and development where applicable.

● Pioneer product testing

Products go through different levels of testing before they are ready for the market. Product giveaways are a good opportunity for you to introduce new products into the market, especially before rolling out a full-scale launch. This is ideal for feedback purposes, so you can go back to the drawing board and tweak a few things factoring in the reviews, then prepare for a big launch.

● Free publicity

Good publicity will do wonders for your product. Come up with a strategy that can help your customers see the product in a good light. Depending on how you prepare and distribute the free gifts, you could get some good publicity. Today all it takes is someone to capture your free distribution on their phones, share it on their social media accounts and your brand will be rocking the airwaves.

At the same time, exercise caution because the average customer today is internet savvy to some extent. Therefore, they can easily dismiss obvious attempts to make your brand or product famous, which could have the entire plan failing.

- Trusted, confident brand

By the time you give free gifts to customers, you believe your product will stand the test of time. You trust that your customers will find and appreciate utility in the product they receive. This level of confidence easily rubs off on your customers too. You are boldly engaging them wherever they are because you trust in your product.

Considering these factors, the benefits of offering free samples outweigh any concerns that you might harbor. Work on a suitable distribution strategy and you can look forward to an incredible promotion drive for your business.

Possible Challenges When Using Free Samples

For all the goodness you can expect from free samples, you should brace yourself for the unsavory possibilities. It is wise to prepare for the worst, but be optimistic about the future. The following are some challenges you might experience when using free samples:

- Business location

The physical location of your business might work to your disadvantage. Some free product promotions are best suited for unique locations with high traffic. Traffic might also vary on a daily basis, and could be influenced by random occurrences like change in the weather. Even with solid plan, this might affect the outcome of your giveaways, and have you extending the promotion longer than you intended.

- Time and money constraints

You will invest a lot of time and money in giving away free products without an implied assurance that your investment will be earned back. For skeptics, this is one of the reasons why free giveaways might not be appealing, hence the need to consider other promotion alternatives.

- Lack of customer assurances

Customers might get your product, but there is no assurance that they will use the product, or even if they do, that they will use it as intended. You might end up giving away free products to people who don't need them in the first place.

If you need feedback from your customers about the products, some customers can lie about their experience to get you off their backs. If you rely on such feedback for decision-making, your decisions will be flawed.

- Predictability

The promotional techniques that people use are often predictable. When the element of surprise is gone, customers lose enthusiasm about the product and the brand. As a result, they assume you are giving away free samples because your products might have an inherent problem.

● Attracting freeloaders

One of the challenges of using free gifts is that you encourage freeloaders to anticipate your next promotion. This is not good for business. Some customers can collude to buy your promotion threshold just so they can get more freebies.

Essentially, product giveaways are a brilliant idea, especially when you have it down to a science. Understand your customers and the market demographics. This is necessary to eliminate or reduce the risk of a loss-making giveaway. People love free gifts. Maximize on this by offering relevant, genuine value and your customers will fall in love with your brand.

Chapter 4
Running A Successful Marketing Campaign on Social Media

"Content is fire, social media is gasoline."

- *Jay Baer*

Is Your Business Social on Social Media?

All businesses today have a social media presence of some sort. This is important to enable them to interact with as many customers as possible. Brand engagement is something you cannot do without today. Through different social media platforms, you have a chance to engage millions of people and widen your reach.

If you don't have an active social media presence, you are missing out on a lot of opportunities. You might have a sound marketing team, but without social media skills your brand is losing out on many golden opportunities. Social networks are currently the best place for lead generation and driving sales.

There are many activities involved in social media marketing, including sharing and posting photos, videos, updates, and any other content that spurs engagement. Beyond what you post on your social accounts, you can also use paid social media advertising to promote your business.

You need a good social media marketing plan, just like any other campaign. Many people assume that all you need for social media marketing is an internet connection and some posts. This might be true for your personal account, but for your business, you have to go the extra mile. Invest in your social media marketing adequately for the best results.

Planning involves coming up with an outline for the marketing campaign. What are your business objectives? What do you want to achieve at the end of the campaign? Social media marketing is a tricky affair because there are so many metrics at play. Without a plan, you would be no different than an excited child in an amusement park without supervision. To help you plan your social media marketing strategy, here are some issues you need to think about:

- Do you have a target audience?

- Why do you need this campaign?

- What is the best hangout place for your target audience online?

- What message should your target audience get from engaging your brand?

These questions will help you work on a clearer strategy for marketing your business online. Besides them, the type of business you run should also help you narrow down your choices.

If you run a marketing agency or any other company that engages in B2B leads, LinkedIn or Twitter would be a good place for you to focus your strategy. The demographics on these networks indicate a high probability of interacting with professionals.

If you own a restaurant, an online store or a travel agency, Pinterest or Instagram are a good option since most of your social media posts will be visual content. These networks are perfect.

Whichever the case, you can still find a way to use all the networks at your disposal. People live different lives on different social media platforms. You may find an individual who is strictly professional on LinkedIn, but is so outgoing and adventurous on Instagram and Facebook. You just need to figure out a way to balance your interaction, investment and engagement with clients on the platforms you prefer.

Why should you invest in social media marketing for your brand? Each business has unique goals. The following are some of the reasons why promoting your business on social media is a good idea:

- You get to build and drive conversations about your brand.

- This is a good opportunity to build your brand identity.

- Creating awareness about your business, offers or products.

- Social media is a good place to generate organic traffic to your business.

- Improve communication with your customers.

- Make your brand reachable by breaking down possible accessibility barriers.

If you can grow your audience and keep them engaged regularly, you will have made a crucial step toward promoting your business.

Tips for Promoting Your Business on Social Media

One lesson you will learn from social media marketing is that the size of your business hardly matters. People will engage you online based on the nature of content you share. Your creativity will earn you major points in this regard. Below are some guidelines that will help you start a promotional campaign for your brand:

● Brand identity

Each social media platform has unique demographics. Resist the urge to copy and paste the same content on different platforms. You can convey the same message using different tones on different platforms to appeal to your target audience. This gives the customer an opportunity to engage your brand at a level they are comfortable with, on each platform they are active on.

● Have a content planner

You don't just wake up one day and decide to post something on your Twitter page then disappear for days. You need a content plan. Social media is like any other marketing avenue. Your plan should include researching keywords and topics that attract your target audience. You also need to study how other businesses are engaging customers on social media. You can learn a thing or two from the competition.

● Shared content

Do you have other content outside social media that might benefit your promotional strategy? If so, use your social media pages to promote them. You can do this by sharing links to such content on your pages. Go through the content and make sure it is suitable for the target audience. The idea here goes beyond promoting your business online. It is also about creating trust in your audience and showing them you are well-read in the subject you are discussing. This confidence boost will help your business, and you might even get other content providers reaching out to share their links with you.

● Importance of quality content

If you have been in marketing for a long time, you must have come across the age-old statement, *"Content is King!"* You need quality content to attract customers and drive conversations online. People lead busy lives, the last thing they want is to come online and get bored by a brand.

The kind of content you are churning out should be consistent with your brand. Consistency is also about the frequency of your posts. Customers are looking for reliability. Regular posts show the customer that you are active online, in which case they can be certain you will respond to their issues when they arise as soon as possible.

● Promoting content online

Your social media platform is a good place to share your best content. This is what your readers, fans, and followers are looking for. The first struggle is usually building a huge fan base for support. Once that is done, you need to engage them to keep them hooked. You can only manage this with quality content. Combine social media marketing with quality content marketing and you will love the results.

● Reputation management

One thing that businesses can never do without is controversy and crisis. At times the causes are beyond your control. Social media gives you the platform to stay ahead of the story. Answer questions customers have, address their concerns and provide answers to those who seek clarity. You must be genuine as you go about this, or it could also backfire and cost you dearly.

- Monitor the competition

What are your competitors doing online? Is there something you can borrow from their strategy to support your promotion? Monitor your competitors to determine what keywords they are using and make arrangements to do the same too. Is their marketing technique working wonders for them? You can do the same, but try and improvise so you can get better results than they did.

- Data analytics

Other than engaging audiences, social media is a good place for data analytics. It is only when you track and analyze data metrics that you can know what really happens when customers interact with your brand pages. There are several tools available for this. Google Analytics is one such tool, though there are other tools available that provide deeper insight beyond what it does.

Through data analytics, you can determine which of your social media campaigns are paying off and which ones you need to dump altogether. This way, you can increase your investment in a specific strategy based on the results. This will also help you determine which social media platform is delivering the best returns, hence an indication of where your target audience is.

Many businesses don't quite know how to handle social media marketing, especially since they have never thought of it as a serious platform beyond socializing. Following the guidelines above, you can use social media to turn your fortune around in terms of promoting your business.

Common Social Media Marketing Mistakes

If you do it right, social media is an engaging platform that can help you grow your market share, increase your ROI and improve your brand visibility. However, people make mistakes all the time, and with social media, such mistakes can be costly in the long run. Social media marketing has been around for a while now. During this period, there are lots of mistakes that people have made when promoting their brands which you can learn from. Let's have a look at some of them below:

- Making assumptions

One of the challenges that many people have when marketing brands on social media is that they assume a lot of things. You assume you are offering your customers the best experience, without following up or conducting research to determine whether this premise is true or not.

Social media is a powerful tool that helps you connect your target audience to your brand. You should not take anything for granted. It can build and ruin your brand at the same time, depending on how you handle interactions with customers. Most of the time brands struggle to get the expected results because their strategies are either outdated, or irrelevant to the target audience.

- No strategy

Not having a marketing strategy is a common rookie mistake. Posting updates whenever you are free is not the best way to go about social media marketing. You would be surprised to learn that a lot of brands still don't give social media marketing the value it deserves. They might even have an intern to manage their social media accounts without supervision. This creates a problem for the company because there is no professionalism in that approach. Over time, these companies end up having to spend on damage control when the intern uses the company account for their personal posts, or engages in some unsavory exchanges on the network.

You must have a strategy for each promotion. Everything else comes after this. Your strategy is not just about the number of posts you upload daily, it includes other things like the right time to post, the nature of content, specific hashtags, or links to share.

- Blind progress

Another mistake many brands make is that they promote their products on social media a lot, but they never track the progress. Without tracking, how do you know the impact of your input? How do you know which campaign was effective?

There are tracking tools you can build into your campaign which will help you make important decisions as your campaign rolls on. You can track engagement, determine the right time to upload photos or videos, the best day for press releases or the best day to promote an offer.

- One strategy to rule them all

Each social network is different. The strategies you use on Twitter might not work on Facebook or Instagram. Even by design, each social network targets different kinds of people with unique interests. Many brand managers make the mistake of using one strategy across all the networks where they have accounts. This is the perfect recipe for disaster.

You have to treat each network as a unique entity. Come up with an independent strategy for each of them. You might borrow a few ideas from one and use them to build a strategy for the other, but make sure your strategies are unique, and align with the basic structure of that network.

● Embrace criticism

People talk about accepting criticism all the time, but never follow their advice when managing social media platforms. Your social media handle cannot be filled with positive comments all the time. In fact, some customers tend to avoid brands that have five star ratings everywhere because it sounds too good to be true.

Resist the urge to delete negative comments from your profile. Some customers will take note when their complaints are deleted, and raise an issue in different forums online. This way, everyone assumes you don't respond well to criticism. Instead, address the issues arising. Reach out to the customer and find out more about their concerns then sort it out.

● Ignoring comments

Your social media page is not a billboard. You are supposed to engage with customers online. Respond to their questions. Read and respond to as many comments as possible. Without this, people feel your brand is disconnected from the conversations they are having about you, in which case they see no need to contact you in the first place. After all, you will never respond to them. This creates a bad reputation for you.

Comments are one way of increasing engagement on your profile. If you have a team working on it, make sure they respond to comments as soon as possible. If you are doing it on your own, set a time to respond to comments and provide as much information as the customer needs. On Facebook, for example, customers can see how frequently the brand responds to messages even before they send you a message.

- Unclear target audience

Who is your target audience? Have you clearly defined them? What makes you believe they are the right target audience? You can communicate with a lot of people online, but not all of them are your target audience. If you don't know who your message should be targeting, all your hard work will be futile.

Remember that other than engaging in discussions, you are also trying to generate leads to your business. Create a personal profile of your target audience, define and describe them to the finest details, including their preferences, age group, gender, where they live, and their interests. From here, you can reinvent your social media strategy and target those who will engage with you and possibly reach out to make a purchase.

How to Position Your Business Online

Millions of people access social media every day. How do you tap into this to position your brand? If you have a business but you don't have a presence online, you are already on the losing side. Soon, your customers and potential customers will move on to a sociable competitor.

One of the challenges that many people have with social media is not whether they are using it, but how to use it effectively. There are lots of tricks, strategies and tips that you come across which might leave you all but confused. The following are simple techniques you can use to make your brand visible online:

- Value addition

Customers love to buy from brands that offer value. They need to see how your product will transform their lives. This is what convinces them to commit to the purchase. Many brands make the mistake of forcing purchases down customers' throats. It feels like shouting at customers to buy your products. No one likes that.

Prove to the customer that they are missing out on something great. Entice the customer, seduce their desires and make them confident in your brand. Once they trust you, they can willingly make the purchase. Don't throw ads everywhere hoping to get buyers. People have tools today to block ads. When you engage them, they won't mind seeing your ads.

- Engaging the audience

Each time you are online you notice lots of videos in your feed. Social media trends keep changing all the time, and at the moment, people are more excited about videos than text or photos. In one video you can communicate so much and move the masses than you can in a photo or a text post. Even the social media algorithms have evolved in light of this dynamic shift in user preferences. Videos enjoy prominence over other forms, and this is something you can use to prop your brand online.

● Managing traffic

Targeted social media advertising is a good way to improve traffic to your business especially if you have an ecommerce business. With millions of users on social media daily, advertising on social media can help you get good traffic leads. This is one of the best ways of converting traffic into purchases.

● Influenced brand awareness

Social media influencers are your best bet to move the masses. You can work with celebrity influencers if you have the budget for it, or find local influencers who can also deliver results. The influencer network is also experiencing an evolution at the moment.

Traditionally, brands would opt for influencers with a huge following online. While that still works, many brands have started looking for influencers who have a handful of followers, but have a deeper and stronger engagement. Such influencers might not have millions of followers, but the few thousand followers they have are loyal.

Influencer marketing is the best way to reach out to customers on social media. Their followers adore them, or hold their opinions in high regard. An endorsement by such an influencer is all your business needs.

Each brand has unique problems that are holding them back. Analyze your current situation. Look at the challenges affecting your business then work on a way to position your business on social media by addressing those challenges. More importantly, social media allows you a lot of room to experiment, and in the process you can learn more about what is best for your brand.

Targeting the Right Audience

For all the talk about targeting the right audience, how do you define your audience? How do you know this is the right group for your sales pitch? Each social network has unique metrics, therefore, you have to use a different approach to find the right audience on each of them. The guidelines below should set you on the right path:

● Target definition

Defining the audience is the first step. There are many factors that you consider in this. Your audience is a person. Imagine yourself describing someone you know, for example, your best friend. Describe the things they like, their preferences, where they love to hang out, their favorite food or even their dream holiday destinations.

It might have taken you a while to list all the things you can use to describe your friend. Imagine doing that for strangers whose only connection to you is your brand. List all the possible preferences you expect of your audience, then start filtering them. This exercise will help you overcome one common challenge: assumptions. Don't assume anything. Customers and their preferences are as diverse as the animal kingdom beneath the sea.

● Segment the audience

Within your wider target audience, you can create sub-groups of categories you can target for different products. Say you are in the fragrance business. You can't sell the same fragrance to everyone. Some people love fruity scents, others love their scents subtle. If you bundle them together in one group, one set of buyers will be alienated.

Segment your audience in terms of the things they are passionate about. Learn more about the customers to determine important metrics like the best time to post content for each group, the kind of campaigns they respond to or the time they are most active online.

● Bring in the influencers

An influencer is like a tour guide. They know the territory better than you do. Discuss your performance, needs, and goals with them. You should have gone through several influencer profiles by now to determine which one among them might be perfect for your business.

More importantly, you need an influencer who is passionate about your brand or your products. It would be absurd to choose an influencer who pushes any kind of product for the money. Such influencers are not reliable, and over time, people lose interest in their work. Customers need influencers they can believe in, people who are loyal to the brands they advertise.

● Monitor conversations

You are investing a lot in this campaign, so it is important to be informed of what people are talking about. Monitor the conversations going on around you. See what people are saying about your competitors, the market you operate in and the industry as a whole. Analyze your content to ensure you are publishing information that interests your audience.

● Create a content calendar

The final step is to build a content calendar. This will guide you on what you are posting and when. Make the calendar editable so you can add and remove content from it as your promotional needs change over time.

Engaging and Maintaining Your Audience

Once you have locked in the target audience, the next thing you should think about is how to maintain them. This is usually the difficult part. Customers' needs change all the time. If they feel your brand no longer satisfies their needs, they will move to someone who does. The same tactics that worked for you might also be used by your competitor. Some customers also like to experiment with different brands all the time. Maintaining your audience is therefore not an easy task. The best you can do is to keep engaging the audience. Below are some guidelines to help you achieve this:

● Appeal to their needs

You keep an audience engaged by uploading content that they love. Data analysis is one of the important aspects of social media marketing that will help you in this regard. Study the kind of content your audience engages with and use that to determine the best topics to discuss.

● Solve problems

Listen to your customers. You will come across several questions that need answers. Solve those problems and share your input on how they can avoid similar problems in the future. Analyze the complaints and concerns customers have expressed over time. You might notice a trend in the kind of problems many people have. Address them and help the customers have an easier experience with your products.

You can also use this chance to upload instruction videos or share links to tutorials and how-to posts that address similar issues. Customers will not just come to your page to buy stuff, they will come for the educational value in it.

● Inspirational content

There's too much negativity on the internet today. People are dealing with a lot of challenges in their lives already. An inspirational post from time to time might just help someone get through their day. A word of encouragement in the morning will inspire the next person just as it sparked some light into your day. At the same time, remember that you are running a business, so don't get carried away and forget your core objective.

The moment people can engage with your content, it is easier for them to keep following you. The relationship between customers and brands is like a parent and a child. Children learn to trust and depend on their parents as they grow. They come to their parents whenever they need information about something. This is the kind of relationship you are fostering with your customers. Don't just treat them as fans and followers, they are people. Relate to them online as you would in person, and your audience will keep growing.

Chapter 5
Investing in Charities and Causes in The Community

"You have not lived today until you have done something for someone who can never repay you."

- John Bunyan

If offered the chance, most consumers would only purchase from brands that they believe are responsible in society. We are not a perfect society. Each community struggles with something, and as a business, this is an opportunity for you to endear yourself to the masses. Over the years, cause marketing has become popular. Companies used to engage in CSR as part of their organizational practices, but today, causes have become a good opportunity to market the brand too.

Cause marketing is a form of marketing where brands engage non-profit organizations and help in financing their cause. The brand can participate by offering financial support, donating items, sending some of their team members to volunteer in the NGO's activities or any other practice that would be welcome.

It is a way of giving back to the community that has served the business and seen it thrive. Cause marketing is perfect for both the business and the cause it supports. The cause benefits from your marketing resources while your brand benefits from exposure to the community. Everyone involved in cause marketing benefits, hence the increasing popularity.

Cause marketing depends on the relationship between the community, the cause, the organization and the brand. Your business objectives, mission, and vision should align with the cause you are supporting. It works even better when you support a cause that your customers and staff are happy about too. It is about building or strengthening your relations with the community you do business with.

Your objective is to encourage more customers to support the cause. They can donate their time or money to the cause. Other than asking for help, you can also use the opportunity to create awareness about the cause, and use it to highlight some of the philanthropic work you have done in the past. Communities that engage in such projects usually hold the partnering brands in high regard. They feel you don't just do business with them, you grow with them. You show concern about the challenges the community is suffering from and you help them find solutions.

Why Should You Support a Cause?

Social impact is a conscientious issue customers keep asking of the brands they engage all the time. Other than taking their money in exchange for your business, what more are you doing for society? After all, your employees are part of that community. How are you making life better for them, and by extension their community?

Don't be discouraged if your brand is not as big as Samsung. You can do big things in a small way too. What matters is not how much you spend, but the appreciation from those who get assistance from your brand. The following are some reasons why you should find a cause you can support today:

● Specific target audience

The cause you support might help you get closer to your target audience or introduce you to a new audience you never acknowledged before. Each cause brings you closer to different customers, many who might never have used your products before, but would be willing to do so given that they love the work you do in their community.

● Lasting impressions

Cause marketing has a deep psychological impact on your customers. They feel good when buying from a company that cares about the environment or their society. They know that part of the money you earn from them goes back into developing their community, and this makes them happy to buy from you.

● Build healthy relationships

This exercise is about more than just supporting a cause. It is also about helping you build healthy relationships with your customers. Such relationships are built on trust, confidence in your business, and integrity.

● You beat the competition

There is no better way to beat your competitors than having the community backing your business. Competition is cut-throat today and through cause marketing, you can position your brand better than the rest. Customers are more likely to purchase from a company that supports a cause dear to them.

Today, cause marketing is more than just your brand's CSR initiative, it is something the community expects of you. If you are not doing something for the community, your competitors are probably beating you to it and a lot more.

Choosing the Right Cause to Support

As your business grows, so does your resource allocation. It is time for you to give back to the community. For this initiative to work, you must choose a charity whose goals align with your beliefs and values. This way, you will be excited about supporting the cause, instead of using it as a conduit for advancing your promotional objectives. The following guidelines will help you find a worthy cause to invest in:

● Research widely

If you have a team, ask them to recommend some causes you can support. Request that they share their reasons too. This way, you know why the cause is dear to them. If you have many entries, have the team vote on which causes you can support. You can also take time and research on some challenges affecting the community around you. You will find worthy causes you can invest in.

● Personal attachment

Look for a cause you believe in. A good place to start would be something you care about deeply or you have a personal connection to. Lucky for you, there are lots of organizations in every community. You could support an education fund, an environmental conservation drive or any other cause. If you have a personal attachment to the cause, you will appreciate the value and time you devote to it.

● Charity begins at home

One of the best ways to support a cause is to find a local organization. Local organizations are ideal in that you see and live the impact of your support each day. The community interacts with your business and the cause you support on a daily basis, which is a constant reminder that you are not just doing business with them, you are also building the community and making it a better place for everyone. Sponsoring students to school might help a few students each year, but the lasting impact on society is incredible.

● Consider the impact

You have been in business for a while, so you know how to factor in returns from investments, and the impact you expect from any money you spend. The same approach applies when dealing with causes. When you have a list of causes you can support, go through the list looking at the overall impact. How many people are affected? How long does it take for the beneficiaries to realize the impact of your investment? Is your investment enough? Do you have to invest monthly or annually?

● Your own cause

If you are struggling to choose a cause to support, why not start your own? This is also a good initiative. You can even have a team devoted to running and championing the cause locally. Talk to the social or community officers and find out some of the challenges they realize when going about their work. You can learn so much from them, and use this as a guide on what you can do for the community.

Effective Cause Marketing Techniques

Cause marketing is great for strengthening your brand's presence in your community. Everyone who interacts with your brand through a cause you support is inspired and encouraged to keep working with you. If you have employees, they are inspired to see their efforts paying off in society too. How can you effectively market the cause you support? Below are some methods that brands have used for years. You can find a technique that suits your business model.

● Cause supporter

The cause supporter initiative is a straightforward method. Your business donates some money to a cause, and from there you can promote your business as a supporter of the cause. Some non-profit organizations even have logos and banners that you can use on your business once you become a partner, like World Vision. Any customer who has donated to World Vision, for example, will be happy to do business with you because they believe you share similar interests.

● Percentage contribution

You have come across this when shopping before. You buy a product and find a label on it that one percent of the sale is donated to a charity organization. Buyers will appreciate this because they feel they are part of something big. You can donate a portion of the sale to an organization that offers scholarships, so each customer knows they are funding an education program for needy students in the society.

● Involve customers

Another good alternative is to involve your customers in the donation process. This works when you have several causes you are supporting. Have a list of organizations you work with, and let the customer decide which organization they wish their donations will be sent to. This is a good option because you provide the customer variety. They might not feel strongly about your preferred cause, but at the same time, they might find a cause they support on the list, probably one that they work with regularly.

● Buy and give initiative

This is another method that is becoming more popular today. In this option, customers can buy two items from your store. While they take one home, they donate the other to a charity organization. Another way to do it is to pledge to donate an item for every product the customer purchases. This approach shows the customer that you care about the cause, and their purchase goes toward a good initiative.

● Incentivize donation

This is a method where you encourage customers to donate to a cause. With each donation, they are entitled to a reward they can redeem whenever they come shopping. This could be a coupon or a discount or any other reward you can give them.

● Match the customer's offer

In this technique, you can work with your customers and encourage them to donate to a cause you support. Once their donation drive is over, you do the math and match their donation in kind. If the customers raised $500,000, you contribute a similar amount to the cause either in cash or a different kind of donation.

Many customers today are willing to engage businesses that are responsible. If you can support a few causes dear to your customers, you have a better chance against the competition. This way of giving back to the community will help promote your brand and ideals and endear you to the community your business operates in.

Chapter 6
Establishing Healthy and Reliable Referral Networks

"Get closer than ever to your customers. So close that you tell them what they need well before they realize it themselves."

- Steve Jobs

Of all the promotional methods you can use to market your brand or product, none has as personal an impact as referral marketing. This is basically word of mouth marketing. It is a powerful technique because the recipient depends on a recommendation from someone they know intimately. More often, they have witnessed the individual using your product so they already love the outcome even before they use your product.

Referrals drive a lot of sales because they involve interactions between real people who know one another at different levels. People recommend products to each other all the time. The loyalty and trust behind referral marketing is stronger than you would experience in the traditional forms of marketing. Instead of relying on a random sales executive to buy your product, the customer believes in the word of their siblings, friends or colleagues who have used your product already.

Most successful referrals come from people the customer knows intimately, but this is not always the case. Think about influencer marketing. Influencer marketing is a pure form of using referrals.

Influencers command a great following online. Their followers interact with them daily and believe in their work and brand endorsements. Many people book their holidays in foreign countries after reading the reviews on TripAdvisor from strangers. Referral marketing is about authority. If the person recommending a product is deemed an authority in the field, it is easier for people to follow their counsel.

The Secret Behind Referral Marketing

Why do people believe in referrals even if the recommendation comes from a stranger? How can you use this mode of marketing to promote your business? Referrals are built around the following factors:

- Unique targets

The audience in a referral marketing program is very specific. Products are often recommended by people you know or trust. You probably wouldn't know about the product without the recommender. They also would not recommend it if it wasn't working for them, or if they didn't believe it could help you as it helped them.

To promote your business, therefore, your objective should be to find people who are associated with the individuals in your target audience. You can start with their friends, for example. When people realize they share common interests in a product online, it is easier for them to engage the brand. They might also reach out to one another and discuss more about how the product is working for them. This strategy works, particularly for personal use products and services.

The audience in referral marketing is usually refined and broken down to very fine demographics. You end up with several niche clusters within a niche. Such segmentation makes it easier for you to penetrate the market and address customer needs intimately.

- Loyalty and trust

Referrals are built on trust. The opinion of someone close to you carries more weight than the opinion of a random ad you find online. Referrals from people you know carry more weight because you have known them for a long time hence you trust their word. You can't buy this kind of trust.

TripAdvisor is one example of a company that has grown over the years by providing reliable reviews about hotels and holiday destinations all over the world. You might not know the people commenting on their experiences, but you trust in their responses because you can read comments going back a few years and see that the hotel lives up to expectations. You can also read the negative reviews and see how the hotel responded to them. When you are done, you trust that you will have an amazing holiday and you proceed to book your stay.

- Wide reach

The tentacles of referral marketing have the furthest reach in the world. In light of social media, a referral can impact your business even in places you have never visited before. For an online company, you might even get business leads from countries you never imagined you would conduct your business in, prompting you to expand into that market.

Each person online has a network of friends that goes beyond anything you can imagine. Their friends have friends and the web keeps growing. If someone shares a review about your business in a fan page or a group the news keeps growing beyond their list of friends and family members. All it takes is a split second.

Building a Referral Network

The first step is to get your customers on board. People who have used your products will share the benefits easily. Encourage them to share their experiences with their peers, friends and family members. While at it, encourage them to talk to you about their concerns when using the product. Your response to the issues raised will make them refer people to your business confidently. Your business can enjoy unprecedented growth during the period when you have the referral program running. The steps below highlight how you can build a reliable network:

● What's in it for the customer?

Just because customers are satisfied with your product doesn't mean they will refer people to your business. You can entice them further by offering incentives. Make sure the incentives are reasonable. A considerable discount will definitely encourage the customer to refer other buyers to your business. The incentive should be reasonable enough for the customer not to pass it up.

● Market the program

People need to know about your referral program to join it. Whenever customers buy something from you, let them know about the referral program. Other than that, try and market the program on social media and any other outlet you use. The best way to go about this is to promote the program as you would a new product line.

● Eliminate complications

You are running a referral program, not a treasure hunt. Try to ensure the program is quite simple. It should be so simple a seven-year-old can use it effectively. If this is not the case, refine the program until it meets your desired specifications. If customers struggle to send people your way, they will not just give up on the program, they might also assume you intentionally make the program difficult so they can't take advantage of the offers.

● Employee induction

Educate your employees so that they are aware of the program and the rewards customers expect. It would be absurd when a customer lines up to claim an offer but the person managing your store is unaware of the same. They should not just be aware of the referral program, they should understand it and be part of it.

Compared to other marketing techniques, referrals are efficient in converting leads to sales. They have a personal touch that appeals to prospective customers better than conventional promotion techniques.

How Your Business Benefits from Referrals

What is in it for you? Why should you have a program that makes your customers brand ambassadors advocating for your products to the people closest to them? There are lots of benefits you stand to gain from referral networks as we will see below:

● Building on trust

Customers trust the people referring them to your business. They are more likely to buy from you when they share a personal connection with the referral. This level of trust cannot be bought, or delivered by any other form of marketing. The new customer does not just trust their referral, they also trust your brand by extension.

● Engagement boost

Referrals give your business a stronger and wider presence in your market. Each time someone is referred to your business, there is chatter about it online or offline. You will also have new users who frequently check out your website for more information or new products. Such visits can easily turn into purchases.

● Widen your market reach

Since the customers are your brand ambassadors, your business outreach is as unlimited as the depth of your customers' network. Traditional marketing might not compare brands directly by highlighting the flaws in a specific brand, but customers are free to talk about such differences without risking a legal tussle. Therefore, they can openly discuss the benefits of your product over a named competitor and convince one another to switch allegiance.

● Customer retention

Ideally, referral marketing helps you create a community of customers. You have a network of people who started using the product after a referral and the network keeps growing. Given the nature of their introduction to your brand, most of the customers will stay loyal to your brand for a long time. Besides, it is easier and inexpensive to retain customers who came on board through referrals than it is to prospect for new customers.

- Manage anticipation

Referrals follow your brand because they are already excited about the journey with you. Their opinion of your brand could not be any higher. From this perspective, you welcome a group of customers to your brand who are happy to buy from you. This is different and better than new customers who experiment with your product before they commit. Referrals don't experiment. They come in ready to commit long-term.

Possible Challenges in Referral Marketing

In as much as referral marketing helps to drive sales among other benefits, you cannot be blind to some of the challenges you might experience going forward. Anticipating challenges will help you plan in advance and have procedures in place to mitigate some of the risk incidents occurring. The following are some challenges you might experience with referral marketing that will affect the possibility of success going forward:

- No one likes your brand

This is a painful experience, but at times the bitter truth is better than a sweet lie. It is an opportunity for growth! Review your engagement with customers over a given period. How would you rate their uptake for your business? How are your sales projections in the weeks or months preceding the referral campaign? If you notice you are not moving as many sales as you used to, the answer might be in your primary product or service.

Find out why people don't like it anymore. Is there a new competitor who is perhaps giving you a difficult time? Have your performance standards dropped for some reason? Get to the bottom of it, and find out what you can do to impress your customers. Once you win them over, you can use them to bring in more customers.

- Unappealing campaign

What are you offering customers in your referral program? If the offer is not appealing, no one will take it up. Just because you are offering something to the customer doesn't mean they appreciate it. Research and ensure the offer is appealing and exciting enough for a customer to consider sharing the information with someone they know.

Your referral program might be failing because you are offering a product or service that customers generally don't like. Besides, if the customer's expectations are not being met, no amount of referral bonuses and offers will work. You must first ensure the original customer is happy, then entice them to share their happiness with others.

- Unknown campaign

This might seem like a simple concern, but its effects are far-reaching. Many times companies have referral programs that their customers are unaware of. Some of the employees might not even be aware either. If they don't know about it, how can they use it to help your promotion strategy?

The best way to enlighten customers about your referral strategy is to use every possible access point to talk to them about it. Inform them online, when they check out, or when paying for goods at your local outlet. Use every means possible to ensure they are aware.

Some outlets you can consider include your autoresponder emails, social media pages, email signature, and official purchase receipts. Don't stop there either. Follow up with the customers and encourage them to take advantage of the program. Highlight the benefits in store for them.

● A complicated program

Naturally, if the referral process is too detailed, many customers will never complete the process. No one wants to be put through a rigorous experience when they have already spent their money on your product. Why do they need to fill a lot of forms? Why is the referral link too long? Why are they being redirected to another website instead of completing the referral in one click? Review your referral program and eliminate anything that bothers your customers. Simplify the process and you will love the outcome.

Growing Your Referral Network

Once you have a referral marketing campaign in place, the next step is to help it grow. As the network grows, so does your market share. You must also focus on keeping your customers happy so they don't have a reason to leave your brand for another. The following techniques will help you grow your referral network accordingly:

● Goal setting

Everything in marketing involves meeting goals and deliverables. What was your plan for the referral network from the very beginning? You might have ended up creating a bigger demand than your current supply chain can handle. This becomes a problem because one of your competitors will step up and fill the void.

A referral program is not just about getting new customers. This might be the basic principle, but for quality business growth, you need to dig deeper. Once you have the new customers from referrals, how do you plan to retain them?

If you have other departments in your business like customer support, sales or even maintenance departments, what role will they play in keeping the new customers happy and the older customers happier? Define each participant's role in your referral network and have procedures in place to ensure these roles are carried out effectively.

- Identify your referral pool

While your customers might be going about their ambassadorial tasks effectively, you should not rest on your laurels. Follow up and find out how the new referrals are connected to your customers. More importantly, find out the common traits they share. This can give you an idea of a new source to pitch your brand for possible leads. This is also how you discover new potential markets.

- Refine your leads list

Spare time and go through your list of referrals. Look at the closed leads, your current, and former customers. Try and find out why some of the customers are no longer with you. What could have changed to make them go away? This might help you learn about a flaw in your business, correct it, and prevent other customers from leaving.

From your list, you can see customers who have been with you for a very long time. These are the most loyal customers. Consider them your inner circle. Such customers understand your business and the value they derive from it, and as a result, they would not hesitate to refer new contacts to you.

Your inner circle customers are probably aware of all or most of the customers they have referred to your business. Look at the value of the customers they have sent your way and surprise them with a reward. Since they were not expecting it, the element of surprise will get them excited and have them looking for more referrals.

If possible it is advisable to create a personal link between your brand and customers. They are a true inspiration and you should make them know it and feel appreciated. These are the customers who have grown with your company over the years.

● Timing requests

When is the appropriate time to remind your loyal customers to participate in the referral program? From your data analysis, you have all the answers. Remind them of the goodies in store for them before and during the holidays. Since they have enjoyed the benefits before, convincing them is easier. Some customers are quite nostalgic and will encourage other customers to buy from you, hoping they can get a similar reward from the previous campaign or something better.

● Recommender values

Referrals are personal connotations. Your brand ambassadors should be people who share the same values as your business. Having worked with them in the past, you know you can trust them. You probably have a beautiful relationship with them already. While this is a good idea, you must also be keen on behavioral changes.

Situations change in people's lives and this can affect their behavior toward your brand or your products. If you realize a customer is no longer as effective as a brand ambassador, find a way to drop them comfortably without creating bad vibes. They might not be relevant to your current campaign, but their work for you in the past cannot go unnoticed.

- Referral alerts

Many processes are currently automated. As your business grows, you might not be able to reach out to each customer on your referral list personally. You can automate the referral list so that the customers are informed of current and future programs whenever they are ready.

You can send them newsletters, links to your blog or product updates so they are aware of what's in store for them. If possible, you can hold referral meetings or webinars with them to teach them about your new products, updates in your referral strategies, the kind of customers you need them to target or any other information that is relevant to your business.

- Track referrals

The size of your business notwithstanding, you must always track your referrals. It is important to know who referred the customers, when and where they met the referral. Such metrics help you strategize future promotional approaches. Did the referred customer buy or make any commitment that requires you to follow up later?

Customer relationship management programs will help you with this. There are many options on the market currently. Find one that is easy for you to understand and use. You can move on to the advanced programs later as your business scales up.

● Appreciation

Your referrers are an important part of your promotional strategy. If you have never thanked them before, you need to make up for it right away. Appreciate their effort. At the end of the year, send them a care package. You can do this periodically if your resources allow.

Don't forget the referred customers either. Thank them for joining your company and working with you. Promise them better things ahead and if possible, give them a hint of some new developments you have in store for them. You need to keep the customers happy. Once you do that, work on keeping your promises.

Conclusion

Everyone needs a voice. By legal definition, your registered business is a person. The business can enter into agreements, contracts, sue and be sued as a legal entity. It has its own identity separate from your individual identity. Your business, therefore, needs a voice too. Through promotional strategies, your business can be heard. Promotional strategies are a window into the world for your business. This is how the business interacts with customers and customers engage the business.

Promotion is a never-ending spectacle. From the moment you start the business, you will engage in different forms of promotion all the time. The business has to grow, and with growth comes effort from your part. While your business is a separate legal entity from your being, it cannot run itself. You have to keep it in check and make sure everything runs smoothly.

We have covered many forms of promotion that will benefit your business in one way or the other. Each of these strategies is effective irrespective of the size of your business. The most important takeaway from every strategy is that it can be done. You simply need to look at your budget and scale the approach according to your resource endowment.

For a sole proprietor, you can handle most of the promotional tasks on your own. However, the biggest challenge you might encounter is finding the time. Remember that your customers do not understand how strained time is as a resource for you. For this reason, create time in your schedule to plan around whichever strategy you use to promote your business. Follow that schedule religiously.

If you run a big company, you have teams in place to handle different promotional strategies. Every strategy is subject to changes and updates from time to time. More importantly, your team is also subject to updates and changes from time to time. As you evaluate the efficiency of your strategies, do the same for your team. You need a team that is efficient and capable of advancing your business objectives as they promote your products.

We have covered a lot of promotional techniques in this book. You are enlightened and excited about the prospects. However, you must also realize that you are marketing for real people, not automated systems. In this regard, understand that customer tastes and preferences change all the time. There will be disappointments along the way - it is a part of entrepreneurship. Do not let the disappointments pin you down. The true test of success is in how you maneuver through these challenges and steer your business toward success.

Anticipate the best outcome, but at the same time, always have a contingency plan in place in case the worst happens. In marketing and promotion, you will experiment all the time. Before you invest in and roll out a strategy for your brand or products, make sure you conduct a feasibility study to see how it works.

One of the highlights that resonates throughout this book is engagement. Engaging your customers is the most important thing in promotion. Engagement is about understanding one another. There is so much that you can learn from your customers and them from your brand.

Many businesses fail because they erect communication barriers between their customers and themselves. Don't make the same mistake. Today there are many communication platforms you can use to interact with customers. Use them wisely and you will have a better chance of growing your business. The last thing customers need is a snobby brand. Put yourself in their shoes for a moment and imagine how you would feel if you engaged a brand that never responded to your prompts. Communication is important in each of the strategies we discussed in this book.

Beyond communication, you must also have a clearly defined target audience. Your promotional campaigns should be channeled toward the right audience. This is an investment in your business. Why waste resources by focusing on people who do not care about your product or brand? Take time and understand who your customers are. Study the demographics and create a customer profile. From this profile, you will know who to target, what their interests are, and where to find them.

The beauty of marketing today is that most of the work can be done on social media. Social media has made work easier for many companies and brands. Even with that knowledge, you should not take social media for granted either.

Creating a profile on your favorite social network is not the end of your work. You have to go the extra mile and build a profile that people can be interested in associating with. If you have the resources, get a professional team to handle social media marketing for you.

Discuss your goals and objectives and agree on the deliverable metrics.

Your business is no longer a hobby, it is a brand. You are dealing with customers who demand accountability from you. A professional approach is mandatory. Interact with your customers as you would investors in your brand. Consult widely in case you are uncertain about anything.

Promoting your business is in itself a product just like the products associated with your brand. You must have an actionable plan of action. Review your plans frequently to assess how effective they are in light of your business goals and objectives. Most importantly, remember that promotion never ends. You simply shift your energy from one approach to another but it never ends.

As your business grows, so does your promotional needs and the importance of refining your strategies to meet the growing demand. This business is your child. Nurture them, teach them, mold them, and help them grow to realize their potential. There is no story more amazing than your success story when your business blossoms into new territories and thrives.

"Would you like me to give you a formula for success? It's quite simple, really: Double your rate of failure. You are thinking of failure as the enemy of success. But it isn't at all. You can be discouraged by failure or you can learn from it, so go ahead and make mistakes. Make all you can. Because remember that's where you will find success."

-   *Thomas J. Watson*

Good luck with your venture!

Bonus Material:
Instagram Marketing 2020

The Playbook for Increasing Your Following and Generating Profits

The Instagram handle that you select needs to be simple. If you have a business website or domain name, then make sure that your Instagram handle is similar to the domain name. It makes it quite easy for others to recognize your Instagram profile. The username must not be vague or obscure. If that is the case, it will be difficult for others to recognize your brand on Instagram. Before you start brainstorming for the perfect username, take some time to learn about all those brands and businesses that failed at growing on Instagram even before they began. Business and brands typically hinder their growth on Instagram when their audience (target and nontarget) are confused and don't know what the brand stands for, identify a lack of cohesiveness throughout the brand messaging and content. Simply put, they realize that the username or profile name doesn't match the content posted on the account.

So, take your time and don't be in a rush when selecting your Instagram handle. It is a great idea to do some research and consult others when brainstorming ideas for your Instagram account. You can ask your family members, friends, colleagues or anyone else to help you along the way. Pick a name that not only suits your brand's objectives, but is also in sync with the marketing strategy of your brand. In fact, you can conduct a quick survey to understand whether or not the Instagram handle you like is the right choice. Why don't you tell a few people about the potential handles and see their first reaction? The initial response is often natural. If they react favorably to it, then maybe you actually have a good Instagram handle in hand.

If you want to use Instagram as a promotional tool, then it is absolutely vital that your Instagram bio is attractive and inviting. Your bio is what will compel visitors to interact with your brand on Instagram. Perhaps, one of the essential aspects of the bio is your brand's username. After all, this is the first thing that your audience will see on your Instagram profile. You must start thinking of ideas that will make it easier for others to find your Instagram profile. Also, you must ensure that the Instagram handle of your brand helps convey your brand's message. The name you choose will depend on the kind of audience you wish to target. It becomes easier to attract your audience's attention when the Instagram handle is unique. If you want to increase your engagement rate on Instagram, a good starting point would be to get creative with your Instagram handle. In this section, you will be given a couple of tips that you can follow for creating the perfect Instagram username.

Think About Your Hobbies

A good Instagram handle usually tells the visitor something about the brand other than its name. This comes in handy, especially if your brand is associated with any form of hobby. By doing this, you're making it easier for your audience to associate themselves with your brand. It also increases the chances of acquiring more followers. For instance, let's assume that you are a brilliant chef named Danielle. There are bound to be several people named Danielle in the world, so you need to come up with an Instagram moniker that will set you apart from the rest. Don't just think about displaying your regular name, instead think of ways in which you can directly associate it with what your page is about. If your Instagram page consists of posts about recipes, the food you cook, and so on, then the username must convey the same. Maybe you can try something along the lines of @crazychefdanielle, or @danisdeliciousfood. You can get as creative as you want with the username.

A Name Generator Tool

You can undoubtedly sit around and brainstorm until you get a perfect idea. However, this isn't always easy, and it can be rather time-consuming. Also, you might not even come up with a good idea after hours of brainstorming. The good news is that there are various online name generating tools that you can use to get started. Even if you get a little idea by using these tools, it will give you some momentum. There are various online username tools like The Cool Name Generator, Spinxo, Screenname Generator, or even Rum and Monkey. In fact, a quick Google search will help you with this. Even if you don't like any of the suggestions given by these tools, you will certainly get some ideas along the way. Most of these online tools require you to enter a couple of keywords along with specific personal characteristics for generating different usernames. Once you make a list of all viable options, the selection process becomes easier.

Use Your Name

You can create a unique Instagram handle by combining different words. At times, having an uncommon name might work in your favor. You can play around with your name and come up with a unique handle. You can try combining your first name and your last name and use it as your Instagram handle. It may or may not work, but spend some time and try rearranging the letters in your name to form a unique handle. For instance, the famous tennis player Serena Williams launched her own clothing line Aneres. Aneres sounds quite exotic and inviting. The name of the clothing line is merely Serena spelled backward. You can do something like this too.

Think About Your Audience

When you're thinking about your Instagram handle, think about the audience your brand caters to. Create a name that will give your audience an idea about what your brand stands for. By doing this, it also enables you to stand apart from the rest of your competition and increases the rate of engagement. Additionally, it becomes easier for your audience to find you. Spend some time and research trending keywords or hashtags related to your brand industry. You can use the Instagram search feature to do the same. While selecting certain keywords, keep in mind that they are not being used by your competitors. You can choose keywords that are associated with the products or services your brand offers.

Unique Characters

You don't have to restrict yourself just to the letters of the alphabet and can also include other characters or numbers into the handle. There are various symbols which you can use like @, #, $, * and so on. However, don't go overboard with these unique characters. Remember that the handle must be easy to find and remember. If the handle is a complicated combination of various characters in letters along with numbers, you merely make it difficult for your audience to find you. You can also use characters for creating emerges which can be placed in your Instagram handle. Even a common name can be jazzed up with a couple of unique characters.

Location

If you have a local business, then it is a good idea to include your location in the handle. Your potential customers might be interested in looking for a specific product or a service in the given area. By adding your location to the Instagram handle, you're making it easier for your potential customers to identify your business or brand. It doesn't mean that you simply include the name of the city in the username. At times, it might even make sense to include the name of the country or even the state. For instance, the famous clothing brand Forever21 has different Instagram accounts for each of the countries it is present in. By doing this, Forever21 is making it easier for its customers to find the Instagram handle that's relevant to them.

Using A Title

If you have a professional title, then you can try adding it to your Instagram profile. Adding a title can certainly help distinguish your brand from others. Ever heard of Dr. Phil, Dr. John, or Dr. Dre? What is the one thing that all these people have in common? They all have a title added to the name. Regardless of whether they are real doctors or not, the title does help. If you are a professional, then try adding your title to the Instagram account. It not only makes the username seem more distinguished but also seems to have a nice ring to it. Don't use a professional title if you don't have one and don't try to trick your followers into believing that you're someone you are not.

Competitor's Profiles

Coming up with the perfect username will undoubtedly take some time and effort. However, if you feel like you hit a roadblock or need a little bit of inspiration, then start checking out the Instagram profiles of your competitors. Make a list of all the people who are popular in your industry or niche and check their profiles. A quick search on Instagram must help you do this. You cannot steal your competitor's profiles, but it will undoubtedly give you an idea or some motivation to come up with a different name for your own profile. At least it will provide you with a starting point.

Duplication Of Names

While creating an Instagram handle, a common problem that a lot of users come across is that after finding the perfect name, they realize that it's already taken. Given that there are billions of people in this world, it is quite likely that someone else might have had the same idea as you. If you come up with a seemingly perfect Instagram name firebrand, and it's already taken, don't worry about duplication of names. Anyway, Instagram will not allow two users to have the same username. So, it is time to get a little creative and modify the username such that it isn't a perfect replica of an existing username. Let us assume that the username you want to opt for is @clarklewis, but you realize that it is already taken. Now, you can try adding a couple of different characters to the basic username to make it different. For instance, you can try, @clarklewi$ or @clark.lewis.

Using Adjectives

Another creative way to create a good handle is to add a few adjectives. Maybe you can opt for a specific attribute, which perfectly describes your brand. For instance, if you are an Instagram blogger who offers relationship advice to women, then @sassysasha sounds better than @Sasha. So, take some time and come up with a couple of adjectives, which describe and lend character to your brand. Once you have a list of adjectives, come up with creative ways of adding to them to your Instagram username.

Additional Tips

The Instagram handle you choose must be easy to pronounce. A person must be able to repeat it without having to write it down. It must be easy to understand and must not be ambiguous. If any part of the name is confusing or is vague, it will merely hurt your reach on Instagram. Keep in mind that if your username is quite similar to an existing username, it can lead to copyright infringement issues. So, be careful while you're trying to imitate another username. Anything too close to an existing username well leads to unnecessary legal trouble.

Another thing that you must keep in mind is that the username must not be lengthy. Regardless of whether it's a profile for a brand or a personal profile, it needs to be short and specific. Adding a word like supercalifragilisticexpialidocious to your Instagram handle is not a good idea. If the name isn't easy to pronounce, how will anyone remember it? Also, a short name offers a certain degree of exclusivity.

Avoid using any names that are related to a specific gender, ethnicity, religion, or sex. If the name seems biased, once again, it will only land you in hot water. The username must not offend or be biased toward anyone. Also, don't make the handle too common or generic. You can certainly combine a common word with a unique word to come up with something exciting and appealing, but don't try to make a generic name your Instagram handle.

Initially, it might seem a little tricky to come up with the perfect handle. The first thing that you must do is stop stressing about it. By following these tips, you can undoubtedly come up with a unique and creative username.

Check out our Other *AMAZING* Titles:

1. Day Trading for Beginners: The Psychology of Day Trading for Beginners

The Ultimate Guide and Tactics on How to Earn a Living through Day Trading for Beginners

"Those types of investments don't come around very often." – John Paulson

There are many different investment strategies, and depending on the sector of the economy you are investing, some strategies work better than others. Day trading is merely a catch all for a style of trading that involves extremely short term investments. Day traders are at an advantage because they are made fully aware of their existing trading balance by the end of each trading day. For example, a day trader will know at the end of each day whether or not he or she has made a profit. It is this type of instant feedback that is emblematic of the entirety of day trading. It's fast-moving, fast acting, and profits are made just as quickly as they are lost.

To best explain day trading, I just want to walk you through a typical day of mine. It's important to note that I have days when I am trading and days when I am not. On the days when I am trading, I am fully focused on trading and have set aside a full six to eight hours to dedicate to trading. Day trading requires focus and your entire attention – the problem is that many traders believe that since they are working from home, they can participate in chores, picking up the kids from schools, and do work outside of trading. The truth is that this is a dangerous path to go down. If you are working on something other than trading during trading hours, you are at a huge disadvantage. The reasons for this drawback will become more obvious as you continue reading, but in short, it limits your ability to cash out at the right time, which is a cornerstone to successful day trading.

When I know that I am going to spend my day trading, I wake up around seven thirty so that I have enough time to analyze what picks I want to make before markets open. With the styles of day trading that I've adopted, styles that you will soon learn, there are three markets on which I can trade – FOREX, penny stocks, and the large exchanges. All three of these offer opportunities for profit and each requires a vastly different trading style to be successful. What is handy about day trading is that since it is so math-based, I don't need to be especially worried about the entire nuance between these different markets. I simply have to adopt the proper strategy to the right market and start monitoring, which brings about the most important aspect of day trading – making your picks and knowing when to cash out.

In an average day, I make around ten to twelve bets/investments. I spend the first ninety minutes to two hours of my day looking for each one of these investments and base them off of a series of tools that I will explain later. What you need to know for now is that I use a series of tools to identify investments that have had high but consistent volatility in the last few days of trading. Volatility is a key principle to day trading and is a measure of how much movement has been on a particular investment. As a day trader, you need to seek investments that have very high volatility. The reason for this is that you are making investments for such a short period that you will need rapid changes to see any profit. In our business, it simply does not make sense to hold onto an asset for a long period of time.

The type of research that we do for selecting stocks is based on *immediate* information. For example, if a press release were to come out saying that Apple expects growth early in 2020, but expects losses for quarter one of 2019, then you can bet that I won't be trading Apple for that day. What other investors see as an opportunity to buy Apple for cheap in 2019 and then sell it in 2020 when it has increased in value simply does not make sense for a day trader. We are operating on the principle of short term cash flow, and even when an investment seems promising, it is not worth the hassle if it is going to take a year or more to pay off. It does not imply that you cannot make these investments on the side, but that for the pure drivers of making money each month, longer-term investments are not the go-to for day traders.

After I have found the investments that I will be making for that day, the rest of the day is dedicated to finding an ideal time to cash out. Finding when to sell a stock is more complicated than simply looking at the ticker price of a stock and deciding what is an adequate profit. Depending on the market and the type of liquidity that you can expect, waiting for the ticker to hit an ideal price means that you may have already waited too long.

To phrase the problem simply for right now, imagine that you were interested in buying a stock when it was climbing in value. Now suppose that you notice the general arc of the climb has started to fold, meaning that even though it is increasing in value, it is not increasing at nearly the same rate that it was even just a few minutes ago. What this does is tell the investors that they should wait to buy the stock, and this is true even if the price of the stock never goes down. The reason is that the liquidity starts to solidify for assets like these, making it harder for sellers to get rid of their stock. As the slowdown approaches, the buying power for those seeking to take a position in the stock increases. Essentially, the potential investor in the stock has more purchasing power than myself, attempting to sell the stock. This is why it is so important to find the ideal time to cash out your investments, and why constant monitoring of the market is necessary when you are day trading. You simply cannot make your investments and then take a relaxed position until it is time to sell because what makes or breaks traders is the exact timing of when they sell their investments.

At the end of my trading day, I typically have released all of the assets that I purchased that morning. Depending on the market, I may have picked up several assets and dumped them during midday, but for myself, I find this to be pretty rare. It is far more common for me to make my initial investments at the beginning of the day and then stick with them for the rest of the trading period until I sell them off before closing. You will on occasion run into situations where it is to your benefit to hold an asset for more than a single trading day, but these are altogether extremely rare, and a specific set of circumstance would have to be met for this to be truly beneficial. The end goal of my trading day is that at least three-quarters of my trades have been beneficial. You need to understand that you will not be successful one hundred percent of the time, but what is important is that you make more successful trades than unsuccessful ones overall.

Day Trading Rules

There are four-day trading rules that every trader should live by. These rules are: never invest for the sake of making a trade on your 'trading' days, always enter a position with a detailed analysis for why you entered, always have an exit plan for every position that you take, and analyze all of your past trades periodically. If you can follow these four rules, which can be difficult to abide by every single day you trade, I'm sure that you will be a successful trader.

The first rule is to never trade simply for the sake of investing on a day when you know you will be monitoring the market. It may appear as a simple rule, but if you experience multiple days where you cannot find suitable investments, it starts to become tempting to make an investment simply to see if it will pay off. The temptation is that you have an investment account and that every day that you do not use it, you are potentially losing out on opportunities for profit. This can be such a tricky feeling to avoid, and it often leaves investors with investments that simply do not benefit them in any real way. The worst-case scenario of this is when an investor invests thinking that it is sound but in reality, does not pass all of their basic requirements from the get-go, but they have no other options, so they trick themselves into thinking it is a good investment. The only way to make sure that you avoid this fate is to always double check that the investment you are going to make is being made for the right reasons and never simply because you know you will be trading that day.

The second and third rules very much go hand in hand. You must have an approach and exit strategy for every position that you take, no matter the market. This means that you know precisely when you are going to enter a position based on past trends. You have a pre-arranged price for a commodity at which you are going to buy it, and you agree that when it is above a certain rate, it is simply not worth the investment. The second part of this strategy is to have a pre-arranged exit price. This has to do with the basic rule that as a commodity is about to peak at price for a trading cycle, it becomes much more difficult to unload. There are tools to help you determine when the market is starting to slow down and when you need to sell, but the best strategy is to simply determine the average volatility of a commodity and sell an asset when it is on the way up before it peaks and long before it starts to fall. For example, let's say that I expect the price of a stock to change by about thirty percent in a trading day. I know this from research and data showing the last few trading cycles on this stock. I have a pre-arranged buy-in price that is determined by the historical lows of the stock over the last few days and also has a pre-arranged sell price based on what I can expect the stock to reach as its expected maximum value for that trading day. This selling price is often before the thirty percent expected change, since the closer the asset comes to its peak price, the harder it becomes to sell.

The last rule to note is that you must keep a trade log with all of your investments. This is a hard strategy to stick to because it requires a lot of extra work on your part, and often the benefits of this work are months away from becoming realized. The trade log that you should keep is a repository of all of the trades that you have ever made, along with specific information about why you made particular trades. For example, in your trade log, you would want to specify basic information, such as the shares bought or sold and the sale and buy price of a commodity. You will also want much more detailed information, such as what tools were you using to identify the commodity as having sufficient volatility to invest, what was your gut feeling on this investment, did you sell the stock at the right time, etc. This is invaluable information because it helps you realize all of the mistakes that you make when trading. A perfect trader does not exist, and often the mistakes that a trader makes are unknown to them because they cannot see beyond the strategies that they have adopted. With a trade log, you can see that certain tools will be more effective for you versus other traders. Most of this narrows down to the fact that as a day trader you will be making a lot of very fast decisions. You need to be more than just able to use tools for stock analysis; you need to be able to use these tools very quickly. This means that you won't have the time to always use basic metrics to determine your picks. With a trade log, you can see which tools you used most effectively, and which you will need practice with. It may seem like you could just pick up on this information yourself, but the truth is that you will be making so many trades per week that you will merely lose track of what was effective and what wasn't. This is the importance of the trade log – it opens your eyes to information that would otherwise stay hidden within a sea of past trades.

*Want to read more? Check out our book on **Day Trading for Beginners** on Amazon today!*

2. Passive Income Ideas For 2020

A Step by Step Guide to Easy Passive Income Ideas For 2020 and Beyond

The best time to plant a tree was 20 years ago. The second-best time to plant a tree is today.

Chinese Proverb

Drop shipping has recently gained traction in the passive income space. It has especially been very profitable because of people's love for online shopping. Here, you as the seller have a website, but you don't necessarily own the product you are selling. It is like a brokerage between the customer and a third-party seller. You never see the product because the product is directly shipped from the third-party seller to the client. The third party here is a wholesaler or a manufacturer. You as a drop shipper never handle the inventory, therefore, reducing the need for a physical location as with usual retailers.

How Does Drop Shipping Work?

The first thing to notice is that Drop shipping is a service that is provided to a customer by a person behind a computer. The manufacturer produces items for sale but doesn't sell directly to the final consumer. This is because it rarely makes any financial sense to sell an item at a time if they deal with millions of products at a go. They offer their products at a lower price in bulk and have little to no purchase requirements, making it convenient for retailers with a lot of capital and wholesalers to buy directly from them. The wholesaler buys from the manufacturer and then raise the cost a little higher to make a profit. They also sell most of their products in bulk as opposed to a single item. The end consumer, therefore, can purchase items whatever the number from a retailer. The retailer buys from a wholesaler and raises the cost even higher to cater to their profit margins. These are the three groups of people that are available in a supply chain, and therefore as a drop shipper, you are a retailer. The drop shipping model is not visible to the end consumer at all. You as the drop shipper can purchase your products from any of the three groups even if you are a retailer. As long as any of them is willing to ship their products to your end user, they are "drop shipping" for you.

Step 1: Order Placement by Customer

A customer surfs through your niche website and finds a product that they want to buy. You as the merchant gets a message informing you of the purchase. Simultaneously, the customer receives a confirmation message of the purchase. The order is automatically generated by the software and sent via email to both parties. The payment is also automatically processed by a payment software, and confirmations are made to both parties.

Step 2: Order placement to the supplier

The order confirmation message is sent to the supplier so that they can process and ship the order to the customer. The supplier debits the total cost of the item from the merchant's account. Their price will be lower than what is charged by the merchant. The price will include order processing fees, shipping fees and the cost of the item. It is therefore up to the merchant to have considered this when they charged the consumer.

Step 3: Order Dispatch from the supplier warehouse

The supplier boxes and ships the item to customer depending on how fast their service is. All this should be included when marketing to the customer. The merchant's logo, address, and contact number are what shall appear on the box and not that of the supplier. Upon shipping, an alert is sent to the merchant along with a tracking number for the order. They also send an invoice for accounting purposes to the merchant.

Step 4: The merchant informs the customer about the shipment

An email alert is sent to the customer with the order tracking information by the merchant through the store's software. The order is complete at this point.

How to Find Suppliers to Work with

As I said before, the difference between success and failure in drop shipping is a reliable supplier. The end user doesn't know that there is a third party involved in the sale. Therefore you will be the one responsible if the item is not shipped, is damaged or of poor quality. Consequently, one needs to work with a supplier that will work well with your business model. You will also need to differentiate between legitimate wholesalers from posers and scammers. How can you separate the fake from the true wholesalers you may ask?

- They want you to pay them a monthly fee instead of charging you for the items you order from them. A legitimate supplier may charge a processing fee, but it is a reasonable amount, and they explain what they are charging you for so you know beforehand. Legitimate fees you will encounter are order processing fees that are added to each order you make. They will also have a minimum amount of goods you buy as your first purchase to weed out buyers from window shoppers. Instead of buying the items, you can advance them the total amount for an order that will go into your merchant account.

- If they are claiming to be wholesalers and yet they are selling directly to customers. This makes the prices go way up as they want to make as much money as they do if they sell directly to the client. That will eat into your profit margins.

There are many ways in which a merchant can find wholesale suppliers to work with.

1. Getting in touch with manufacturers

If you know the products you want to sell, looking for manufacturers to work with is not hard. All you have to do is finding out from them a list of their distributors. From then you can look for the one that does drop shipping and asks for requirements to set up an account with them.

2. Make use of the internet

The internet is full of information as everyone is advertising online. Depending on your niche, many people offer the service you need. Be careful as you can also encounter scammers. Don't just settle for the first suppliers that you see on the top page. Go deeper into the search engines as many good wholesalers may be hidden in the result searches. Look at the offers as opposed to the design of their websites. Don't give up on the first try and don't expect to get a good wholesaler immediately.

3. Scout, your competitor's supplier

Finding a wholesaler is hard and what better way to get one than good old fashion espionage. You can order from your competitor.

You can call the number on the return address which is more likely to be the supplier.

4. Trade fairs and shows

Many manufacturers go to trade fairs where they network with potential retailers. The trade fairs are arranged according to the products, and you can easily pinpoint manufacturers in your niche. Some are free, and others have an attendance fee. Take advantage of many manufacturers in the same place.

5. Directories

There are many directories in the market that you can look for suppliers in your niche. They include SaleHoo, Doba, Wholesale Central and so on.

Attributes of a Good Supplier

*   Professionalism and experience

If you are new at drop shipping, a professional representative will be able to talk you through the process and assure you along the way. They can also be able to answer your questions on any topic you may have.

*   Around the clock support

Suppliers that answer the client's questions swiftly inspire confidence with the client.

*   Tech-savvy organization

Because drop shipping is done from all corners of the globe, technology is the only thing that is unifying every player in the game. Orders and payments have to be done swiftly and securely through state-of-the-art software to improve customer experience. At the bare minimum, they should have email connectivity.

- Good location

If you are a drop shipper, you may want to look for a supplier that is close to almost all your clients to improve the delivery time while reducing shipping costs.

- Efficiency

A good supplier cares about your customer satisfaction which will guarantee you a repeat customer. They will provide good quality products and handle the shipping process with care and urgency.

How to Pick the Right Product for Dropshipping

Drop shipping is an online business, and the best way to know what people want is to search on the Internet. With SEO, it is easy to understand what people are looking to buy online through keyword searches. You can also see what people in your geographic location, what to buy and then what is in during a particular season. Remember that drop shipping is not a static business and those that evolve make the most money.

Consider the price at which the supplier is offering. The price at which you offer the customer should be reasonable; otherwise, you will need to offer phone support for assurance. The recommended price range for most online customers is $50-$200. Sell a product with a MAP (minimum advertised price) pricing so that there isn't much difference in prices between you and the competition.

Look at the scalability and longevity of your business. Your product should be able to stand the test of time and the tides of trends. Consider how you can market the product to potential customers. Sell things that go together so that the customer doesn't click away from your website. Sell items that do not change with time or perishable goods.

Look at what customers need to find the perfect items to sell. If something can be bought at a local store, then it is not worth the time. Avoid bigger and fragile products as they are expensive to ship and may break down during shipping. Also, avoid items that could be faulty when the customer tests it out. You want to run a business without returns and complaints to keep getting positive reviews.

Advantages of Dropshipping

1. Starting capital is small compared to having a physical location

All a merchant requires is a website to display the products they are selling. They do not need to buy any inventory or storage space to keep it. This reduces the starting capital to a bare minimum. The Dropshipping model ensures that you make a sale first before buying it from the supplier and even then, the burden of packaging and shipping lies with the third party. The cost of running the business is also low as there is no physical store to run. Overhead expenses like rent, employees' salaries, office supplies, and licenses are not something a drop shipper has to worry about. They only need a computer, reliable internet connection and a website to do their business which is monthly services and can be accessed at a low cost

2. It is an easy business to start

Compared to many businesses today, starting a Drop shipping business can be easy. Everything you need to know about running an online business can be accessed online. You can also keep improving your marketing skill after starting the business as there is nothing for you to lose. Compared to business people with an inventory, you don't need to worry about stock taking, office management. As you will not be handling any inventory, the stress of replacing finished products, packing and shipping orders to clients or getting a warehouse is not yours. Making sure orders get to the clients and dealing with returns is also someone else's business.

3. You are not bound to any location

You can start a Drop shipping business anywhere in the world as long as you have a laptop and a strong internet connection. With the availability of large e-commerce stores that can help you connect with manufacturers directly, you can do business with anyone in the world today. Payments can also be made online without the merchant, customer and the manufacturer ever meeting face to face. All you need is trust and reliability coupled with connectivity to the internet.

4. You can sell a wide range of items

A standard retailer worries about space and cost of purchasing inventory when deciding what they want to sell. This is not the case with drop shippers. All they need to do is check if the client has the product in stock and then they put it up on the website for sale. A drop shipper can have different categories and selections for different customers as long as the third party can supply it to the customer.

5. It takes a short time for the new business to scale upward

The problem standard retail model is that with more customers, the processing of orders increases and thus the need to hire more stuff. This burden is absent in this case as, despite the increase in orders, it's the supplier that deals with packaging and shipping. This doesn't affect the merchant in any way except maybe making payments more frequently which hardly seems like a con. The other work that may increase maybe in customer care but that can be solved with one employee or two.

Disadvantages of Dropshipping

1. Some niches have low-profit margins

Depending on the niche that you choose to go into, there is the possibility of making a little profit per item. In the beginning, the merchant may under-price to get traffic to the website. He or she will have to sell a lot of products so that they can make more money in the long run which can take a while to happen. There is also a lot of competition online, and the customers will end up picking the website that offers the lowest price.

2. You have to choose the right supplier

Unless you have the utmost trust that your supplier will deliver the products to the customers at the right time and in the right condition, your business is bound to fail. Standard retailers don't face this problem as they can assure quality control in their inventory and shipping process. You will, therefore, need to experiment until you get the right partner. Customer complaints will most definitely be directed towards you despite the mishap not being our fault. Ensure you communicate with your suppliers constantly to improve the shipping process and reduce complaints.

3. The challenges of dealing with multiple suppliers

As a drop shipper, it isn't uncommon to deal with many suppliers at the same time. Some may be dependable, but some may not, and the customer may buy items that come from different suppliers. First, there may be significant differences in shipping costs that may not make sense to the customer. Computing different shipping charges from different suppliers may be hard because the cost may be too much for a customer to handle. You may, therefore, have to standardize the charges which may come from your pocket.

Despite being an easy way to make passive income, Drop shipping requires a lot of dedication and hard work. It is not a get rich quick scheme. These challenges can be overcome if the merchant uses different strategies from everyone else.

*Want to read more? Check out our book on **Passive Income Ideas** on Amazon today!*

www.ingramcontent.com/pod-product-compliance
Lightning Source LLC
Chambersburg PA
CBHW021942190326
41519CB00009B/1108